RESEARCH
IN THE PSYCHOBIOLOGY
OF HUMAN BEHAVIOR

Adolf Meyer

Research
in the Psychobiology
of Human Behavior

Edited by

EUGENE MEYER III

Professor of Psychiatry and Medicine
The Johns Hopkins University School of Medicine

and

JOSEPH V. BRADY

Professor of Behavioral Biology
The Johns Hopkins University School of Medicine

The Johns Hopkins University Press
Baltimore and London

The Johns Hopkins University Press, Baltimore, Maryland 21218
The Johns Hopkins Press Ltd., London

Library of Congress Catalog Number 78-24710
ISBN 0-8018-2238-6
Library of Congress Cataloging in Publication data will be found on the last printed page
of this book.

CONTENTS

PREFACE

The Adolf Meyer Symposium on Psychobiology was organized to mark the centennial of The Johns Hopkins University and to honor the man who was the first Henry Phipps Professor of Psychiatry and founder of the first medical school department devoted to the development of the basic behavioral sciences as applied to neuropsychiatric disorders. The papers that compose this volume were presented as part of that symposium and provide a view of current frontiers in psychiatry and behavioral science from the perspective of Meyerian psychobiology. We believe the research strategies and findings will prove of value to today's medical students, to physicians in academic psychiatry, and to those interested in disciplined research in the various fields of human behavior.

It was in 1915, two years after the opening of the Phipps Clinic, that the term *psychobiology* become part of the title to a published paper. It was Meyer's generic designation for a disciplined scientific study of man. Characteristically, the title adds, "with subordination of the medically useless contrast of mental and physical."

The psychobiology of Adolf Meyer not only provided the title and focus for his lectures and discussions with the medical students but was in reality nothing less than his exposition of the biologic and social origins of consciousness. To this continuing effort Meyer brought his expertise as neuropathologist, a conviction of the importance of man's personal and social history, and the recognition of speech and language as central to the understanding of human behavior in health and in disease.

Adolf Meyer directed his own laboratory of neuropathology and in this setting offered experience for students, staff, and visitors in gross and microscopic anatomy of the brain. His publications in this field ranged from detailed drawings of the comparative neurology of the neocortex of vertebrates

vii

to the labyrinthine interconnections in the cerebrum concerned with audition and its processing to the motor areas of speech behavior. Thus he made tangible and operational his conceptual integration of the central nervous system in relation to behavior. Not content with what he called a "mind shy" behaviorism, Meyer appointed Horsley Gantt, student of Pavlov, as head of a laboratory to explore further the role of conditioning and learning in laboratory animal behavior. Curt Richter was appointed to conduct a broad range of studies emphasizing biologic influences on behavior in animals and in man. The Pavlovian Laboratory and the Psychobiological Laboratory of the Phipps Clinic have flourished even to the present day as a result of this typical Meyerian foresight, and the professional ranks of clinical psychiatry were enriched by the products of the Phipps residency program. The fruits of that unique training experience have continued to be in evidence through the contributions of Wendell Muncie, Franklin Ebaugh, Thomas Rennie, Alexander and Dorothea Leighton, Maurice Levine, Theodore Lidz, Jerome Frank, and many others.

By 1937, the twenty-fourth anniversary of the opening of the Phipps Clinic, students and colleagues of Adolf Meyer occupied substantial numbers of the major teaching posts in psychiatry in the United States. Recognition of his contributions extended to important circles of European psychiatry, particularly through Sir Aubrey Lewis, chairman and professor of the Institute of Psychiatry of the Maudsley Hospital in London, and Sir David Henderson, professor and chairman of the Department of Psychiatry at the University of Glasgow.

How, then, can one describe briefly how this and much else came to pass? Historically, one must understand the happy coincidence in 1912 of the needs of The Johns Hopkins Medical School in bringing the basic sciences to bear on clinical medicine and Adolf Meyer's personal commitments, his self-elected training, and the directions of his intellectual curiosity. Meyer had come in 1892 from Switzerland, the smallest democratic state, to the United States—even then the most sprawling and multidirected, and certainly the largest, democracy in the world. The then prevailing climate of opinion in the United States was one of optimism as to what scientific empiricism might bring to the general welfare of mankind. This faith in rationalism found ample basis in the impact on society of such inventive genius as that of Thomas Edison, Alexander Bell, and the Wright brothers. In medicine, this faith in science and technology found more modest but still powerful impetus from the Flexner Report, which advocated development of the basic sciences in the training of physicians.

These strong hopes for the specific and general benefits of science and technology were expressed by the most influential thinkers of the late nineteenth and early twentieth centuries in the United States. Among these were William James, the philosopher and proponent of pragmatism, and John Dewey, philosopher and educator, who maintained that "science is the organ of social progress." In the field of history, Frederick Jackson Turner was espousing the influences of the expanding geographic frontier on the general American culture. In politics and economics, this period was the historical high-water mark of action-minded individualism whether conservative, liberal, or radical in outside dress. Whether the influences were personal or through the writings of these progressive thinkers, there is no question of their impact on, or congeniality with, Meyer's own conceptualizations.

It was in this setting that Adolf Meyer pursued his studies of neuropathology, which he systematically related to the clinical histories of those patients whose brains he examined so carefully. In a patient who had received a gunshot wound to the head, Meyer first discovered and described radiations from the optic nerves running through the temporal lobe to the optic cortex, fibers that came to be known as "Meyer's loop." Clinically, interruption of these fibers resulted in a homonymous hemianopsia. This was also the period in which the brain lesions of central nervous system syphilis were first discovered and related to behavioral disorder.

Despite his own expertise and a general enthusiasm for "organicity"—an enthusiasm that analogized from the lesions of paresis to possible explanations of all neuroses and psychoses—Meyer was influenced, one must suppose, by his negative neuropathologic findings in many severely disturbed and hospitalized psychiatric patients. By 1906, in any case, Meyer first formulated his views of schizophrenia as disorganization of the patient's life habits. Thus he attributed in such patients a highly significant etiologic role to neonatal experience while not denying the possibility of genetic or metabolic contributing causes. In the same paper he advanced his essential monistic view of the inseparability of physical and psychological causes, a view reflected in his frequent reference to the etymology of the word *pathology* as "the logic of suffering." By 1910 he had also published his views on paranoid states, a nosological delineation that has remained essentially unaltered to this day.

These major contributions to neurologic and psychiatric thought occurred during Meyer's tenure at Worcester State Psychiatric Hospital and during the period 1902 to 1910 as director of the Pathologic Institute of the New York State Hospitals. These contributions no doubt made him the outstanding candidate, in the view of William Welch, professor and chairman of the Department of Pathology at Johns Hopkins, for appointment as the first full-time chairman of the newly endowed Henry Phipps Psychiatric Clinic. Adolf Meyer occupied this position from 1913 through 1941.

At Johns Hopkins, Meyer established courses in undergraduate psychiatry throughout the entire four-year medical curriculum. Time scheduled for education in psychiatry soon came to equal that for teaching in medicine and surgery. It included optional opportunities to learn brain anatomy and pathology as taught by Meyer himself. Work in the laboratories of Horsley Gantt and Curt Richter, as well as electives in clinical psychiatry and neurology, were also available to students. The intersection of psychiatry with the community at large was brought home to staff and students in a busy outpatient department run by Dr. Esther Richards and through student visits and clinical collaboration with the Spring Grove State Hospital. In all, it was a program exposing everyone concerned to teaching in neuroanatomy, physiology, biology, and genetic-dynamic psychiatry and to the community in which it all took place.

This program was, in fact, a living representation of Adolf Meyer's greatest legacy to psychiatry today—his philosophy of man. Meyer himself might have preferred to describe his work in more modest terms. He might have characterized it as the facts of human development in health and disease and their organized application to the professional care of patients. What was lasting in Meyer's philosophy cannot be neatly packaged or easily conveyed. Throughout his life he concerned himself with the role of intelligence in human affairs and the part played by biologic development, especially that of the central nervous system, in the potentialities and limitations of human behavior. One might describe his philosophy as a dynamic humanism with due regard for the part played by ethics but with, to use Meyer's own words, "relatively little urge for the mystical."

Adolf Meyer was above all concerned with expansion of the frontiers of scientific knowledge to include a science of man in his biologic, psychologic, cultural, and historical aspects. Less recognized, but of current significance, was Meyer's emphasis on symbolization, the spoken and written word and conceptual thought as man's unique tool in the perception and mastery of his world. For Adolf Meyer the central importance of symbolization was confirmed in the evolution of the central nervous system in vertebrates. It was dramatically illustrated in the progressive physical enlargement and specialization of the cerebral cortex, which anatomically dictates the uniqueness of man and contrasts with the much smaller size of the neocortex of the old-brain-oriented behavior of infrahuman species. "The development of language constitutes the most distinctive attainment in the progression from dumb animal to man," Meyer once stated, and he added, "Why not look to man's linguistic record in the same way we study his prehistoric bones in paleontology and his cultural record in archeology?" Thus Meyer antedated conceptually much of the current interest in the origin and structure of language. He discussed the etymology of words that indicate higher mental functions—*r*eligion, *r*esponse, *r*espect, *r*egard, *r*esearch—and correlated the origins of these highly meaningful words and the origins of the human cortex in historic linkage with the origin and nature of consciousness.

Of at least equal philosophic importance was Adolf Meyer's emphasis on "spontaneity" in human responses, which he related to the human capacity to grow, develop, and learn and to recover from injury, hurt, and defeat. Just as consciousness was a dynamic expression of capacities of the central nervous system or brain, so spontaneity was an expression of the capacities of man to be aware of himself and his relations with others. Spontaneity in human behavior was for Meyer a biologic fact—essential to a broad confidence in the possibilities of growth and learning, of the appearance of the really new, and of an attitude that expected good as well as evil from uncertainty.

Meyer's views on the importance of spontaniety probably account for his increasing departures from Freud's psychoanalytic formulations, then also in the process of publication. It would appear that Meyer viewed Freud's earlier psychoanalytic formulations of consciousness as too mechanistic and believed that they did not do justice either to the capacities of the central nervous system or to man's behaviors in society. His objections were more than theoretic, however, because they reflected differing views as to the treatability of psychotic patients.

Meyer's philosophy of man is not so much outdated as it is difficult to assemble from multiple sources. Meyer himself had great difficulty in condensing his views on psychobiology; his Salmon lectures, given in 1933 and entitled "Psychobiology," only came to publication seven years after his death in 1950. Since these were the first Salmon lectures, a singular honor, it is probable that Meyer was reluctant to consider his conceptions of psychobiology as ever complete. Publication only came about in 1957 because of the devoted efforts of Eunice Winters, his editorial assistant.

One of the editors of the present volume, Eugene Meyer, was a student of Adolf Meyer's during his last four years as chairman of the Department of Psychiatry; the other, Joseph Brady, holds the professorship of Behavioral Biology at The Johns Hopkins University School of Medicine as a direct descendant of the positions established by Adolf Meyer through his appointments of Horsley Gantt and Curt Richter. Thus we have shared common features of the Adolf Meyer "culture" and have as well had the opportunity to know and evaluate his contributions from somewhat different vantage points.

At the personal level of experience, Meyer's detachment and objectivity were combined with a kind use of wisdom and a quiet, slightly sardonic humor. The very personal roots of this detachment were evidenced in the manner in which he faced the imminence of his own death. A visit with him in 1949 provided a firsthand report of some of the events of his life during his retirement. He first spoke of his work and interests during and just after World War II. "Then came the Brady experience," was his description of a prostatectomy undergone at the Brady Clinic. By his own account, this operation was followed somewhat later by "a small but telling cerebral accident resulting in an interesting thalamic syndrome of emotional incontinence." He was thereby explaining that he now cried when listening to the music he had previously enjoyed. Thus in his personal life, as in his formal teaching, Meyer exemplified a synthesis of the special sciences with a direct grasp of human experience, a synthesis most apt to bring assistance and hope to the sick person.

Above all else, Meyer had an enduring trust in the persuasive power of the truth and its capacity to survive and even thrive in the marketplace of free competition for the minds of men. Meyer believed the first frontier of *mental hygiene*, a term he revived, to be the thorough education of medical students and the continuing education of physicians in a comprehensive and updated understanding of mental illness. The four large volumes of his collected papers represent the diverse but highly elaborate areas of his main interests—neurology, clinical psychiatry, medical education, and mental hygiene. They speak most elegantly for the unique quality of his leadership and for his belief that theory must derive from admitted participation in human living and be susceptible to testing in action.

The field of medicine today is being bombarded by the elaboration of truly amazing and productive technical achievements on the one hand and the impingements of a society in real turmoil on the other. In their efforts to cope with these uncertainties, scientists and practitioners alike can find courage in the teachings of Adolf Meyer.

The editors wish to acknowledge their great indebtedness to Mrs. Patricia A. Thiess. Without her fine editorial assistance and moral support this volume would not have been published.

RESEARCH
IN THE PSYCHOBIOLOGY
OF HUMAN BEHAVIOR

I

NOREPINEPHRINE
MEDIATED SYNAPTIC TRANSMISSION
AND HYPOTHESES OF PSYCHIATRIC
DISORDERS

*Floyd E. Bloom**

Introduction

The psychiatrist whose career we honor in this volume, Professor Adolf Meyer, desired keenly to understand the basis by which individual humans interacted with the cosmos of life in which they lived. He believed that the sources underlying active responses to the probings of the world were to be found in the greater understanding of the biology of the brain. In this sense, he used the term *biology* to cover the general class of scientific facts that pertain to all aspects of the study of life, and not those more restricted topics we generally now cite when we speak of neurobiology.

Admittedly, my own areas of expertise—if any—seem quite remote from the topic of human interaction; in fact, they are at the opposite pole of a logarithmically reduced scale dealing with the question of how neurons interact with the world in terms that can begin to be answered in matters of chemistry and physics. Attempts by my associates and me to integrate the chemical and physical world of molecular neurobiology into some primitive quests for principles underlying the neuronal basis of behaviors generate my comments here.

*Director/Arthur V. Davis Center for Behavioral Neurobiology/The Salk Institute/La Jolla, California

1

In enunciating an explicit approach to a neurochemical pursuit of behavioral regulation through neuronal events, I stipulate in advance that such a monolithic approach to the neurochemistry of behavior is not my intention. The profound exclusionary blinders that might easily be inferred from my obsession with one chemical class of neurons (the norepinephine [NE]-containing neurons of the nucleus locus coeruleus [LC]) are to be taken as an example of how behavioral level events may eventually be viewed in terms of single cell interactions. Like Professor Meyer, we offer suggestions for approaches and not solutions, remaining humble to the ever-unfolding complexities of the brain and its continually evolving strategies for our survival.

Testing the Effects of NE on Brain Activity

The ability of NE to affect the pattern and rate of electrical activity of central neurons has been known for some time (Bloom 1968; 1974 for review). The majority of this data has been derived from studies that employ the technique of microiontophoresis to administer relatively small amounts of NE onto single neurons within the intact brain and that interpret the ensuing functional changes in rate and pattern of discharge or transmembrane properties as evidence of the general role of NE in interneuronal communication.

By proper experimental control, tests with microiontophoresis of NE (Bloom 1974) reveal generally reproducible inhibitory effects of NE on neuronal discharge. However, such responses do not necessarily imply an underlying NE-mediated input to the cells being tested. To corroborate this inference requires the demonstration that selective stimulation of the afferent NE axons will reproduce the effects produced by microiontophoresis of NE. Since the cells of origin for the cortical NE projections have only recently been established, the next best evidence has been to establish cytochemically that the cells being tested received NE-containing synapses. In the absence of such corroborative data, iontophoretic responses simply cannot be interpreted functionally.

Structural Properties of Norepinephrine-Containing Synapses. The varicosities of the axons demonstrated by fluorescence histochemistry indicate presumed sites of transmitter release. However, because of the limited resolution of the optical microscope relative to the very fine nature of the complexly interrelated cellular processes of the neuropil, electron microscopy is needed to determine precisely which neurons in a given region receive synaptic contact from NE-containing axons.

No single electron microscopic histochemical method has yet achieved the consistency and selectivity of localization desired for analysis of NE-transmitting synapses. Permanganate fixation methods (Bloom 1973; Landis and Bloom 1975) offer the most direct approach to the successful visualization of small granular synaptic vesicles, which seem identical morphologically and pharmacologically to the storage vesicles of NE in peripheral sympathetic nerve terminals. Recently we have begun to explore the use of glyoxylic acid as a prefixative for permanganate fixation, and we have also been able to observe small granular vesicles within synaptic terminals in brain (Bloom, Koda, and Battenberg, unpublished).

By application of the combination of fluorescence histochemistry and permanganate fixation, or alternatively by autoradiography of H^3-NE and acute degeneration after 6-OHDA, NE-containing synapses have been identified ultrastructurally in two cortical regions, cerebellum and hippocampus, with defined postsynaptic target cells. In addition, presumptive NE-containing synapses have also been identified cytochemically in squirrel monkey cerebral cortex (Freedman, Foote, and Bloom 1975). These studies provide the structural documentation for the physiologic studies described next, which are pertinent to psychiatric hypotheses.

Action of Norepinephrine on Defined Postsynaptic Neurons

The Noradrenergic Projection to Rat Cerebellar Purkinje Cells. Norepinephrine-containing synapses in the cerebellum can be localized at the electron microscopic level by degeneration after 6-OHDA exposure or autoradiography of sites taking up H^3-NE, as well as by permanganate fixation (Landis and Bloom 1975). These ultrastructural studies indicate that NE-containing fibers synapse on the Purkinje cell dendritic tree, in the mid-to-outer molecular layer. Recent techniques for facilitating visualization of these fibers (Bloom et al., unpublished) suggest that they are of sufficient density to permit contact with each Purkinje cell.

Experiments utilizing changes in formaldehyde-induced fluorescence of neurons and axons in animals with lesions of the ascending NE bundles, or cerebellar peduncles, or utilizing autoradiography after micro-injections into NE nuclei have shown that the cerebellar adrenergic projection arises from the nucleus locus coeruleus (Pickel, Segal, and Bloom 1974a, b), a bilateral group of NE-containing neurons in the dorsal pontine reticular formation.

When NE is applied to Purkinje cells from micropipettes by iontophoresis, there is a uniform and powerful depression of spontaneous discharge

(Hoffer, Siggins, and Bloom 1971). Interspike interval histograms show that NE specifically augments the population of long pauses seen during normal Purkinje cell firing (Hoffer, Siggins, and Bloom 1971). Iontophoretic administration of MJ-1999, a specific beta-adrenergic blocking agent, antagonizes NE responses (Hoffer, Siggins, and Bloom 1971). Intracellular recordings from Purkinje cells during extracellular application of NE (Siggins, Hoffer, and Bloom 1971a) result in hyperpolarization with either no change or an increase in membrane resistance.

When locus coeruleus is stimulated, Purkinje cells show remarkably uniform inhibitory responses: cells recorded extracellularly display depression of spontaneous discharge rate (Siggins et al. 1971b). With intracellular recordings, LC stimulation exactly mimics the action of exogenous NE: both produce hyperpolarization without a decrease in membrane resistance.

The Noradrenergic Projection to Rat Hippocampal Pyramidal Cells. Next, noradrenergic effects were pursued in the hippocampal cortex, a brain region known to receive an extensive input of NE-containing fibers (Segal and Bloom 1974a, b). We have confirmed the presence of NE terminals by fluorescence histochemistry, by 6-OHDA-induced degeneration (Bloom and Segal, unpublished), and by autoradiography after micro-injection of labeled precursors into the locus coeruleus (Pickel, Segal, and Bloom 1974a). The hippocampal NE projections onto pyramidal cells function in a fashion quite similar to the effects of the locus coeruleus on cerebellar Purkinje cells: LC and NE slow pyramidal cell discharge with long latency and long-duration actions; the receptor is blocked with MJ-1999, and the action of the pathway is totally blocked by chronic pretreatment with 6-OHDA or acute pretreatment with reserpine and alpha methyl tyrosine.

Cyclic 3'5'-Adenosine Monophosphate as a Mediator of Norepinephrine Action in the Central Nervous System

In both the cerebellar and hippocampal systems, cyclic 3'5'-adenosine monophosphate (cyclic AMP) was observed to mimic the ability of NE to depress spontaneous activity, and the NE receptor could be blocked by the MJ-1999. Based in part on the pharmacological potentiation of the inhibitory effects of NE, LC, and cyclic AMP on cerebellar Purkinje cells, we have proposed that these actions could be mediated by cyclic AMP (Bloom et al. 1975; Bloom 1975). Subsequently, the proposal has been strengthened by observations that the actions of NE of the NE-pathway and of cyclic nucleotides all hyperpolarize Purkinje cells and hippocampal pyramidal cells (Segal and Oliver, in preparation) through an unexplained membrane action in which membrane conductance to passive ion flow is not increased, as it is with most other known synaptic chemicals (Bloom et al. 1975). Even more direct confirmation of this hypothesis stems from the observation that NE and the NE pathway will selectively increase the immunocytochemical assay of Purkinje cell cyclic AMP content (Siggins et al. 1973). Such post-synaptic mediation for the NE pathways offers several possible biologic advantages, particularly the twofold advantages of (1) biochemical amplifi-cations of the catecholamine signal and (2) the possibility of directly altering the postsynaptic cell through the ability of cyclic AMP to regulate protein and carbohydrate metabolism.

Norepinephrine and Behavioral Effects

Direct electrophysiological tests of the presumptive behavioral function of the norepinephrine projections have been accomplished by direct electro-physiologic recording from unrestrained, unanesthetized cats (Chu and Bloom 1974), rats (Segal and Bloom 1976a, b), and squirrel monkeys (Foote, Freedman, and Oliver 1975). The results of these tests indicate that, although NE directly inhibits spontaneous discharge even more potently than in acute anesthetized preparations, the response to certain sensory inputs may never-theless be increased. Thus, the relative signal: noise ratio exhibited by a specific sensory target cell, in squirrel monkey auditory cortex to specific squirrel monkey vocalizations, is effectively increased because NE produces relatively greater suppression of spontaneous activity than the response to vocalizations (Foote, Freedman, and Oliver 1975).

The effects of the LC pathway have been evaluated with respect to the cellular discharge patterns of hippocampal neurons in awake rats through chronically implanted recording and stimulating electrodes (Segal and Bloom 1976a, b). Under these conditions the pathway shows a longer and more pronounced inhibition of pyramidal cells than observed in the anesthetized rat (fig. 1.1). When biologically nonsignificant but loud auditory stimuli are presented to the rat, hippocampal units generally respond with inhibition: preconditioning stimulation of the LC before such auditory stimuli results in greater inhibition of discharge (fig. 1.2), as might be expected by the algebraic summation of two inhibitory drives. However, when rats are trained to associate the same loud tone with the presentation of a food reward, the tone no longer inhibits hippocampal units, but instead results in poststimulus excitation of discharge. When locus coeruleus conditioning stimuli are now paired with the tone under these conditions, the effect of locus coeruleus stimulation is to enhance even more the "excitatory" translation of the tone stimulus, even though when tested against simple spontaneous discharge in the knowledgeable state the LC pathway is by itself always inhibitory (Fig. 1.2).

These data, plus the well-known ability of chronic electrical stimulation of LC to produce reinforcement of lever-pressing behavior (as reviewed by Stein 1974), strongly suggest that the LC pathway may be employed by the brain to attribute special value to a particular set of environmental signals that can facilitate the execution of approximately rewarding motoric or cognitive responses in reaction to these environmental signals (sleep, eat,

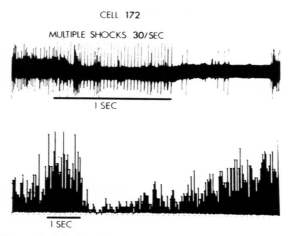

Figure 1.1. Electrophysiologic effects of stimulation of the nucleus locus coeruleus on the discharge pattern of a hippocampal pyramidal neuron in an awake unrestrained rat. A permanently implanted stainless steel wire electrode records single unit discharges in the hippocampus (above) before and during one second of stimulation of the locus coeruleus at 30 Hz (through a bipolar stimulating electrode permanently implanted into the anterior pole of the ipsilateral locus coeruleus). Note that the rapid tonic and bursting discharge of the hippocampal unit is strongly suppressed by the locus coeruleus stimulation and that the effect continues for several hundred msec after the end of the stimulus train. In the lower panel, a poststimulus time histogram illustrates the cumulative inhibitory effects of five successive stimulus trains presented at relatively long interstimulus intervals and the effects followed for seven seconds after each stimulus. (The apparent increased firing during the stimulation period—heavy one-second bar below record—results from incorporation into the histogram of stimulation pulse artifacts. Note that the inhibitory effects of the one-second stimulation train persist for three to five seconds afterward.

Source: Adapted from M. Segal and F. E. Bloom, The action of norepinephrine in the rat hippocampus. III. Hippocampal cellular responses to locus coeruleus stimulation in the awake rat, *Brain Res.* 1976a.

drink, etc.). In fact, when the natural firing patterns of norepinephrine-containing neurons are related to the spontaneous behavior of unrestrained cats, most identified LC neurons appear most active in paradoxical sleep (in a phasic relation to periods of rapid eye movement) and in the earliest stages of awakening from paradoxical sleep (with rapid tonic activity) (Chu and Bloom 1974; Hobson, McCarley, and Wyzinski 1975).

Norepinephrine and Psychiatric Research Insights

The above information from experimental animals provides an initial characterization of the function of NE pathways to two of the many brain targets that receive such pathways (see Lindvall and Bjorklund 1974 for many others). Although the present status of NE in cellular neurobiology may not accurately reflect its function in every brain region in which it occurs, these data do suggest that changes in activity within the neuronal projections of the nucleus locus coeruleus to the hippocampus and the cerebral and cerebellar cortex can influence information processing. Although these norepinephrine circuits normally function to suppress spontaneous activity in the awake animal, the pathway may be more properly regarded as a biasing filter, or modulator circuit, to amplify behaviorally

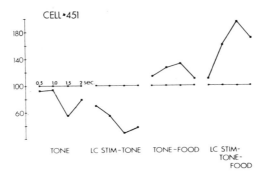

Figure 1.2. Interactions between the experimental activation of the locus coeruleus and the changing effects of a loud tone on hippocampal unit discharge during training. The recording and stimulating electrodes are similar to that described in Figure 1.1; the post-stimulus time histograms have been simplified by expressing the average discharge rate during four consecutive poststimulus time blocks to the one-second prestimulus period. Note that in the second panel locus coeruleus stimulation augments the inhibitory effects of the tone, while in the fourth panel locus coeruleus stimulation is also able to augment the excitatory effects of the same tone after the tone has taken on significance from food reinforcements. When the effects of locus coeruleus stimulation are evaluated on hippocampal firing without concurrent tone presentations, the effects are always inhibitory (as shown in Figure 1.1).

significant afferent signals, perhaps as an initial step in attributing to these sensations a possible reinforcement value.

Such cellular functions may then be theoretically applicable to the analysis of mental disorders in at least two major ways. First, as exemplified by the various monoaminergic theories of schizophrenia, or affective disorders, the primary cellular defect of psychiatric disease could lie primarily in the hypofunction or hyperfunction of one or all of the NE projection systems. Thus, ineffective use of the noradrenergic sensory biasing function could lead to a failure to discriminate between environmentally significant sensory signals and could result in the perceptual inundation phenomena described in schizophrenia (Stevens 1973). Still, the nature of the primary cellular functional defect here requires elucidating experiments to explain how antipsychotics that also are effective antagonists of neuronal responses to NE (Freedman and Hoffer 1975) can restore functional balance to an overactive or a supersensitive synaptic system.

Alternatively, the primary cellular pathophysiology of mental illness might lie in pathways other than the monoamines. In this case, one might presume that the brain normally uses the functional consequences of NE synaptic action (both the biasing and the cyclic nucleotide-producing functions) to attempt to restore the potentially faulty pathways. However, even with this scheme, one must still ask how drug therapy assists in the restoration of the proper degree of functional regulation. Perhaps future experimental emphasis needs to be given to the repeated observations that dysfunctions in brain performance produced by one form of pathology (tumor, degeneration, stroke) can often be alleviated by a second induced lesion (as in ablation of the thalamic nuclei to improve motor function in Parkinson's disease). Is it possible that the anti-NE actions of some antipsychotics are useful through this sort of functional readjustment?

Conclusions

Recently it has been my pleasure to collaborate in a series of studies (Robinson et al. 1975; Robinson and Bloom 1975; Robinson and Bloom, in submission) in which rats have been studied along several chemical and physical parameters after small experimental cortical infarcts have been produced. Associated with such strokes we find reversible changes in some cortical and brain stem transmitters, including NE, as well as reversible changes in behavior. Some of the changes in behavior of the animals could be organized into an animal behavioral dysfunction syndrome that loosely approximates some features of agitated depression. When viewed in such terms and in association with the monoamine hypotheses of affective disorders (Schildkraut and Kety 1967), the experimental situation could be explicable from the notion that the cortical damage results in a much broader hypofunction of the cortical projections of the LC, perhaps as a part of the biological changes that will eventually lead to regeneration of the damaged processes. In accordance with this view, such drugs as amphetamine or desmethylimipramine (which can be shown to release NE or to prolong its extraneuronal transit after release by slowing active re-uptake) also eliminate the behavioral changes of experimentally infarcted rats. In fact, if the cortical NE projections are previously destroyed in total with 6-hydroxydopamine, the same sort of infarct results in no observable behavioral syndrome.

These experiments obviously are far from complete and can still be interpreted in many ways, some of which may be pertinent to psychiatric illness. I summarize them here only to be able to reiterate the views expressed more fully above—that understanding of the cellular changes that underlie interneuronal communication events of behavioral significance may be possible to achieve through the methods of neurobiology. To concentrate on a single neurochemical class is acceptable only at this early stage of the effort when we are able to disregard temporarily all those circuits whose chemistry, anatomy, and function we cannot yet measure. Eventually, however, like Professor Meyer, we biologists must be aware of the holistic functions of the brain in order to elevate our neurobiology to the level of his psychobiology.

References

Battenberg, E.L.F., and Bloom, F. E.: A rapid, simple, and more sensitive method for the demonstration of central catecholamine-containing neurons and axons by glyoxylic acid induced fluorescence. I. Specificity. *Psychopharm. Commun.* 1: 3-13, 1975.

Bloom, F. E.: Electrophysiological pharmacology of single nerve cells. In *Psychopharmacology*, ed. D. Effron. Washington: Government Printing Office, 1968.

————: Ultrastructural identification of catecholamine-containing central synaptic terminals. *J. Histochem. Cytochem.* 21: 333-48, 1973.

————: To spritz or not to spritz: the doubtful value of aimless iontophoresis. *Life Sci.* 14: 1819-34, 1974.

————: The role of cyclic nucleotides in central synaptic function. In *Reviews of Physiology, Biochemistry and Pharmacology*. Heidelberg, Germany: Springer-Verlag, 1975.

Bloom, F. E.; Siggins, G. R.; Hoffer, B. J.; Segal, M.; and Oliver, A. P.: Cyclic nucleotides in the central synaptic actions of catecholamines. In

Advances in Cyclic Nucleotide Research, ed. G. I. Drummond; P. Greengard; and G. A. Robinson. New York: Raven Press, 1975.

Chu, N. S., and Bloom, F. E.: Activity patterns of catecholamine-containing pontine neurons in the dorso-lateral tegmentum of unrestrained cats. *J. Neurobiol.* 5: 527-44, 1974.

Foote, S. L.; Freedman, R.; and Oliver, A. P.: Effects of putative neurotransmitters on neuronal activity in monkey auditory cortex. *Brain Res.* 86: 229-42, 1975.

Freedman, R.; Foote, S. L.; and Bloom, F. E.: Histochemical characterization of the neocortical projection of the nucleus locus coeruleus in the squirrel monkey. *J. Comp. Neurol.* 164: 209-31, 1975.

Freedman, R., and Hoffer, B. J.: Phenothiazine antagonism of the noradrenergic inhibition of cerebellar Purkinje neurons. *J. Neurobiol.* 6: 277-88, 1975.

Hobson, J. A.; McCarley, R. W.; and Wyzinski, P. W.: Sleep cycle oscillation: reciprocal discharge by two brainstem neuronal groups. *Science* 180: 55-57, 1975.

Hoffer, B. J.; Siggins, G. R.; and Bloom, F. E.: Studies on norepinephrine-containing afferents to Purkinje cells of rat cerebellum. II. Sensitivity of Purkinje cells to norepinephrine and related substances administered by microiontophoresis. *Brain Res.* 25: 523-34, 1971.

Landis, S. C., and Bloom, F. E.: Ultrastructural identification of noradrenergic boutons in mutant and normal mouse cerebellar cortex. *Brain Res.* 96: 299-306, 1975.

Lindvall, O., and Bjorklund, A.: The glyoxylic acid fluorescence histochemical method: a detailed account of the methodology for the visualization of central catecholamine neurons. *Histochemistry* 39: 97-127, 1974.

Pickel, V. M., Segal, M.; and Bloom, F. E.: A radioautographic study of the efferent pathways of the nucleus locus coeruleus. *J. Comp. Neurol.* 155: 15-42, 1974a.

————: Axonal proliferation following lesions of cerebellar peduncles: a combined fluorescence microscopic and radioautographic study. *J. Comp. Neurol.* 155: 43-60, 1974b.

Robinson, R. G., and Bloom, F. E.: Reversal of spontaneous hyperactivity following experimental cerebral infarction by treatment with DMI, d-amphetamine, or 6-hydroxydopamine. *Neurosci. Abstr.* 1: 306 (#475), 1975.

Robinson, R. G.; Shoemaker, W. J.; Schlumpf, M.; Valk, T.; and Bloom, F. E.: Effect of experimental cerebral infarction in rat brain on catecholamines and behavior. *Nature* 255: 323-34, 1975.

Schildkraut, J. J., and Kety, S. S.: Biogenic amines and emotion. *Science* 156: 21-30, 1967.

Segal, M., and Bloom, F. E.: The action of norepinephrine in the rat hippocampus. I. Iontophoretic studies. *Brain Res.* 72: 79-97, 1974a.

_____: The action of norepinephrine in the rat hippocampus. II. Activation of the input pathway. *Brain Res.* 72: 99-144, 1974b.

_____: The action of norepinephrine in the rat hippocampus. III. Hippocampal cellular responses to locus coeruleus stimulation in the awake rat. *Brain Res.* 107: 499-511, 1976a.

_____: The action of norepinephrine in the rat hippocampus. IV. The effects of locus coeruleus on evoked hippocampal unit activity. *Brain Res.* 107: 513-25, 1976b.

Siggins, G. R.; Battenberg, E. F.; Hoffer, B. J.; Bloom, F. E.; and Steiner, A. L.: Noradrenergic stimulation of cyclic adenosine monophosphate in rat Purkinje neurons: an immuno-cytochemical study. *Science* 179: 585-88, 1973.

Siggins, G. R.; Hoffer, B. J.; and Bloom, F. E.: Studies on norepinephrine-containing afferents to Purkinje cells of rat cerebellum. III. Evidence for mediation of norepinephrine effects by cyclic 3',5'-adenosine monophosphate. *Brain Res.* 25: 535-53, 1971a.

Siggins, G. R.; Hoffer, B. J.; Oliver, A. P.; and Bloom, F. E.: Activation of a central noradrenergic projection to cerebellum. *Nature* 233: 481-83, 1971b.

Stein, L.: Norepinephrine reward pathways: role in self-stimulation, memory consolidation, and schizophrenia. In *Nebraska Symposium on Motivation*, University of Nebraska Press, 1974.

Stevens, J. R.: An anatomy of schizophrenia. *Arch. Gen. Psychiatry* 29: 177-89, 1973.

II

GENETIC ASPECTS OF SCHIZOPHRENIA: OBSERVATIONS ON THE BIOLOGICAL AND ADOPTIVE RELATIVES OF ADOPTEES WHO BECAME SCHIZOPHRENIC

*Seymour S. Kety**

The mental illness or illnesses that we call schizophrenia constitutes a major social problem in terms of suffering, the loss of human potential, and sheer public cost. Its gravity is matched by our ignorance regarding its causes. It is not surprising, therefore, that hypotheses have taken the place of knowledge, nor that these hypotheses have grown into doctrines and dogmas. The syndrome was first described at a time when the new sciences of microbiology and pathology were making important contributions to medicine, and the natural assumption was made that schizophrenia was a simple disease of the brain that the neuropathologists would soon characterize. That did not happen convincingly, and meanwhile Freud brought a new dimension into psychiatry in the recognition of the importance of life experience, the interaction of a child with its parents, especially its mother; and a new doctrine developed that postulated the overriding importance of "schizophrenogenic" parents in the development of schizophrenia. More recently, a doctrine has emerged that insists that schizophrenia is not a disease of the brain but is a myth devised by the psychiatric establishment, which uses it to label what is a creative adaptation to a sick society. Although the belief in one or another of

*Professor of Psychiatry/Department of Psychiatry/The Mailman Research Center/Harvard Medical School/Belmont, Massachusetts

Table 2.1.
Concordance rates for schizophrenia in studies of monozygotic and dizygotic twins

Author	Date	Monozygotic pairs		Dizygotic pairs	
		N	% concordant	N	% concordant
Luxenberger	1928	19	58	13	0
Rosanoff et al.	1934	41	61	53	13
Essen-Möller	1941	11	64	27	15
Kallman	1946	174	69	296	11
Slater	1953	37	65	58	14
Inouye	1961	55	60	11	18
Tienari	1963	16	6-36	20	5-14
Kringlen	1964	55	25-38	90	4-10
Gottesman & Shields	1966	24	42	33	9
Fischer et al.	1969	21	24-48	41	10-19
Pollin et al.	1969	80	14-35	146	4-10
Gottesman & Shields	1972	20	40	31	10

Source: Compilation by Gottesman & Shields (1972). Same sample as 1966 study but based on blind consensus of six judges.

these doctrines is often very strong, the evidence on which they depend is quite weak.

In the absence of demonstrable biological abnormalities in schizophrenia, belief in their existence has rested on observations that have suggested the importance of genetic determinants in schizophrenia. But that evidence, too, has been inconclusive and compatible with alternative explanations that are difficult to rule out.

Schizophrenia is known to "run in families," and a large number of epidemiological studies attest to an approximately tenfold higher risk for schizophrenia in the siblings, parents, and offspring of schizophrenic individuals than in the general population. But since a family shares not only its genetic endowment but also its environmental influences, either or both of these could be operating to account for the familial tendencies.

Better evidence has appeared to come from studies in twins, and a substantial number of such studies that have been carried out agree in the finding of a high concordance rate for schizophrenia in monozygotic twins, while the concordance in dizygotic or fraternal twins is no greater than that in siblings (see table 2.1 from Gottesman and Shields 1972). Although these observations are compatible with genetic theory, they depend on an assumption that monozygotic twins differ from dizygotic only in the degree of their genetic congruence. If monozygotic twins also share more of their environmental influences than dizygotic twins, it is difficult to determine how much of the discrepancy between monozygotic and dizygotic twin concordance is genetic and how much is accounted for by environmental factors.

Studies with adopted individuals offer a means of minimizing these sources of error. Since an adopted individual receives his genetic endowment from one family but his life experience as a member of another, it may be possible to disentangle genetic and environmental factors by studies based upon such individuals and their biological and adoptive families. If a total population of adopted individuals can be surveyed—in which the occurrence of schizophrenia in the biological relatives occurs after the time of adoption and is not a basis for the transfer, the mental status of the biological relatives and the adoptees is largely unknown to each other, and independent diagnoses in each population can be made without that information—it should be possible to reduce to a minimum many types of selective, ascertainment, and diagnostic bias.

In 1963 my colleagues David Rosenthal, Paul Wender, Fini Schulsinger, and I began to collect a total sample of adults legally adopted at an early age by individuals not biologically related to them. We began with all of the legal adoptions granted in the city and county of Copenhagen from the beginning of 1924 to the end of 1947, rejecting those who had been adopted by biological relatives, yielding a total of 5,483 adoptees. For the purposes of the study, we included as "definite schizophrenia" three subtypes defined in the diagnostic manual of the American Psychiatric Association: chronic schizophrenia, latent (ambulatory or borderline) schizophrenia, and acute schizophrenic reaction. Thirty-three schizophrenic "index" adoptees were selected by independent review of the abstracts of the institutional records of the 507 adoptees who had ever been admitted to a mental institution. Unanimous agreement on diagnosis of chronic, latent, or acute schizophrenia was arrived at among four raters (F.S., D.R., P.W., S.K.). A control group was selected from the adoptees who had never been admitted to a psychiatric facility by matching with each index case on the basis of age, sex, socioeconomic class of the rearing family, and time spent with biological relatives, child-care institutions, or foster home before transfer to the adopting family.

Our first report of prevalence and type of mental illness in the relatives was based simply on an examination of institutional records that were available for the biological and adoptive parents, siblings, and half-siblings of the index and control adoptees. These were identified through the adoption records and the Folkeregister. Abstracts of the hospital records were made, translated into English, and edited to remove any information that would suggest whether a subject was related to an index case or to a control or was a biological or adoptive relative; then an independent diagnosis was made by each of the four raters. A consensus diagnosis was then arrived at by conference among the raters.

We have previously developed the hypothesis of a "schizophrenia spectrum" of disorders presumably related to schizophrenia and including—besides the three forms of schizophrenia we had accepted in the selection of index cases—a category of "uncertain schizophrenia," in which schizophrenia was the best diagnosis that could be made, although from the information we had we could not be certain; and a category of "schizoid or inadequate personality," which appeared to have some of the characteristics of schizophrenia but to a considerably milder extent. A statistically significant concentration of "schizophrenia spectrum" disorders was found among the biological relatives of index cases as compared with those of the controls, while the adoptive relatives showed a low incidence of schizophrenia spectrum disorders for both the index and the control group with no difference between them (Kety et al. 1968). The number of these illnesses we found in the relatives was too small to permit a further breakdown of the schizophrenia spectrum. Furthermore, we had secured little information about the environment of the probands other than the presence or absence of mental illness in their adoptive relatives. One of our other studies (Rosenthal et al. 1968) had also suggested that there were many more schizophrenics and individuals within the schizophrenia spectrum than had ever been hospitalized.

For these reasons we felt that it would be important to carry out complete psychiatric interviews with these relatives, which might permit a more exhaustive survey of the population with regard to schizophrenia and other psychiatric diagnoses and more information about life experience. We secured the collaboration of Dr. Bjørn Jacobsen, a Danish psychiatrist, who agreed to carry out the interviews and spent the greater part of the next two years in doing so.

A total of 512 relatives were identified through the population records. Of these, 199 had died, and 29 had emigrated or disappeared. There was an interesting and highly significant difference in the death rate between the biological relatives of index cases (of whom 35 had died by February 1973 as compared with only 13 among the biological relatives of controls, p = 0.0004). That difference is accounted for by suicide, accidental, and other traumatic deaths. Of the remaining 364 relatives, more than 90 percent participated in an exhaustive psychiatric interview conducted by Dr. Jacobsen, who had not known the relationship of any subject to a proband (see table 2.2).

In practically all of the biological relatives, the subject did not know of that relationship and did not inform Dr. Jacobsen. Extensive summaries of these interviews were prepared, edited to remove any clues that would permit a guess of the relationship of the subject to a proband, and then read in-

Table 2.2.
Status (as of February, 1973) of biological and adoptive relatives*
of index and control probands.

	Biological Relatives		Adoptive relatives		Total relatives
	Index	Control	Index	Control	
Total identified	173	174	74	91	512
Dead or inaccessible	49	25	35	39	148
Died†	35	13	35	36	119
Left Denmark, Sweden, or Norway	13	11	0	2	26
Disappeared	1	1	0	1	3
Alive and accessible	124	149	39	52	364
Agreed to interview	112	138	34	45	329
Refused interview	12	11	5	7	35
Refused but adequate information	6	2	1	3	12
Refused and inadequate information	6	9	4	4	23
Interview or adequate information obtained	118	140	35	48	341

*Parents, siblings, and half-siblings.
†The only significant difference between the groups is that the number of deaths is significantly higher for the index biological relatives vs. control (p - 0.0004) and for control adoptive vs. control biological relatives (p < 0.0001); the latter is undoubtedly a reflection of the age differences. The percentages of interviews granted or refused in the accessible populations are not significantly different (P—Fischer's exact probability).

dependently by each of three raters (D.R., P.W., S.K.). Each rater independently recorded his best psychiatric diagnosis for each subject from a list of possible diagnoses covering the entire range listed in the diagnostic manual (DSM-II) of the American Psychiatric Association, ranging from no mental disorder to chronic schizophrenia. After that a consensus was arrived at among the three raters, the code was broken, and the subjects were allocated to their respective four groups: biological or adoptive relatives of schizophrenic index adoptees and biological or adoptive relatives of control adoptees.

Of these four populations, one is different from the rest in being genetically related to a schizophrenic with whom they have not lived, i.e., the biological relatives of the index cases. With regard to mental illness other than schizophrenia these relatives do not differ from the rest (see table 2.3). Thus this study provides no support for a genetic relationship between organic, neurotic, affective, or personality disorders and schizophrenia.

In the case of the schizophrenia spectrum of disorders and for the individual components with the single exception of "schizoid or inadequate personality," however, there is a concentration in the biological relatives of

Table 2.3

Psychiatric diagnoses outside the schizophrenia spectrum made by a consensus of three raters in edited interviews

	Biological relatives				Adoptive relatives			
	Index	Prevalence (%)*	Control	Prevalence (%)*	Index	Prevalence (%)*	Control	Prevalence (%)*
Total identified	173	...	174	...	74	...	91	...
Complete or adequate interviews	118	...	140	...	35	...	48	...
Interviews without schizophrenia spectrum diagnosis								
Normal	82	...	121	...	31	...	41	...
Organic	30	36.6	49	40.5	11	35.5	11	26.8
Neurosis	7	8.5	6	5.0	5	16.1	6	14.6
Affective disorder	4	4.9	6	5.0	3	9.7	2	4.9
Personality disorder	2	2.4	11†	9.0	1	3.2	3	7.3
Psychiatric diagnosis other than schizophrenia spectrum	27	32.9	39	32.2	8	35.8	15	36.6
	40	48.7	62	51.2	17	54.8	26	63.4

*Calculated as percentage of interviewed relatives excluding those with schizophrenia spectrum diagnosis.
†Prevalence of affective disorder is lower in index biological relatives than in control biological relatives (P = 0.049); for none of the other diagnostic categories in the prevalence significantly different between index relatives their respective controls (p—Fischer's exact probability).

Table 2.4.

Prevalence of schizophrenia spectrum disorders in the biological and adoptive relatives of schizophrenic index and control probands (from consensus diagnosis on interview)

Type of relatives	Number identified	Number interviewed	Schizophrenia spectrum N %*	Schizophrenia Definite Chronic B1 N %*	Schizophrenia Definite Latent B3 N %*	Schizophrenia Definite Total B1 & B3 N %*	Schizophrenia Uncertain D1, D2, D3 N %*	Schizophrenia Uncertain Total B & D N %*	Schizoid inadequate personality N %*
Biological index	173	118	37 21.4	5 2.9	6 3.5	11 6.4	13 7.5	24 13.9	13 7.5
all biological controls	174	140	19 10.9	0 0	3 1.7	3 1.7	3 1.7	6 3.4	13 7.5
screened biological controls†	113	86	11 6.4	0 0	1 0.9	1 0.9	0 0	1 0.9	10 8.8
p‡ (all index vs. controls	...	N.S.	0.006	0.03	0.25	0.026	0.009	0.0004	N.S.
P‡ (all index vs. screened controls)	...	N.S.	0.007	0.08	0.16	0.019	0.001	0.00003	N.S.
Adoptive index	74	35	4 5.4	1 1.4	0 0	1 1.4	1 1.4	2 2.7	2 2.7
all adoptive controls	91	48	7 7.7	1 1.1	1 1.1	2 2.2	3 3.3	5 5.5	2 2.2
Screened adoptive controls†	64	34	3 4.7	0 0	0 0	0 0	1 1.6	1 1.6	2 3.1
P‡ (index vs. controls	...	N.S.	N.S.	N.S.	N.S.	N.S.	N.S.	N.S.	N.S.
P‡ (Index vs. screened controls)	...	N.S.	N.S.	N.S.	N.S.	N.S.	N.S.	N.S.	N.S.

* Calculated as N/identified relatives.
†Relatives of the 23 "screened" controls (i.e., interviewed and found to be free of any suggestion of schizophrenic illness).
‡P—Fischer's exact probability.

Table 2.5.
Schizophrenic illness in the biological paternal half-siblings of schizophrenic
index cases and controls (from consensus diagnoses based upon institutional
records or interviews)

Probands (N)	Number of biological paternal half-siblings	Diagnosis of Schizophrenia					
		Definite		Uncertain		Total	
		N	%	N	%	N	%
Schizophrenic index (33)	63	8	12.7	6	9.5	14	22.2
Controls (34)	64	1	1.6	1	1.6	2	3.1
P* (index vs. control	N.S.	0.015		0.055		0.001	
Screened controls (23)	42	0	0	0	0	0	0
P* (index vs. screened control)	N.S.	0.014		0.042		0.0004	

*P—Fischer's exact probability.

index cases in contrast to the persons who are not genetically related to a schizophrenic. For chronic schizophrenia, the prevalance in the biological relatives of index cases is 2.9 percent compared with 0.6 percent in the other three groups; for latent schizophrenia it is 3.5 percent compared with 1.2 percent; and for uncertain schizophrenia it is 7.5 percent compared with 2.0 percent. For any of these diagnoses of schizophrenic illness, the prevalence in those genetically related to the schizophrenic index cases is 13.9 percent compared with 2.7 percent in their adoptive relatives or 3.8 percent in all subjects not genetically related to an index case (see table 2.4). The difference between the group genetically related to the schizophrenic index cases and those not so related is highly significant statistically and speaks for the operation of genetic factors in the transmission of schizophrenia.

The evidence thus far presented is compatible with a genetic transmission in schizophrenia but is not entirely conclusive, since there are possible environmental factors—such as *in utero* influences, birth trauma, and early mothering experiences—which have not been ruled out. However, there are 127 biological paternal half-siblings of index cases and controls among these relatives who can help to settle that question, since the biological paternal half-siblings did not share the same mother, neonatal mothering experience, or postnatal environment with their adopted half-siblings. The only thing they shared was the same father and a certain amount of genetic overlap. The number of paternal half-siblings is almost identical for index cases and

Table 2.6.
Schizophrenic illness in the biological and adoptive families of
schizophrenic index cases and controls (from consensus diagnoses based upon institutional records or interviews)

Probands	Number of families	Families with one or more members diagnosed as schizophrenic							
		Biological				Adoptive			
		Definite		Definite or uncertain		Definite		Definite or uncertain	
		N	%	N	%	N	%	N	%
Schizophrenic index	33	14	42.4	17	51.5	1	3.0	3	9.0
Control	34	3	8.8	5	14.7	3	8.8	5	14.7
p* (index vs. control)	....	0.002		0.001		N.S.		N.S.	
Screened control	23	1	4.3	1	4.3	1	4.3	2	8.7
p* (index vs. screened control)	....	0.001		0.0001		N.S.		N.S.	

*p—Fisher's exact probability.

controls, but the number of those who were diagnosed as having definite or uncertain schizophrenia is markedly different, 14 among the half-siblings of the index cases and only 2 among the half-siblings of controls (p = 0.001). There is a similar concentration if we restrict the diagnosis to definite schizophrenia (see table 2.5). We regard this as the most compelling evidence we have obtained that genetic factors operate significantly in the transmission of schizophrenia.

These data do not permit the conclusion that schizophrenia is a unitary disorder, since they are equally compatible with a syndrome of multiple etiologies and different modes of genetic transmission. Although the twenty-four diagnoses of definite or uncertain schizophrenia were distributed among the biological relatives of seventeen of the index probands, there were sixteen had no diagnosis of schizophrenic illness in their biological relatives (see table 2.6). The possibility that there are at least two forms of schizophrenia, in one of which there is a strong genetic basis that is weak or absent in the other, would be compatible with our data.

These data do not imply that genetic factors and the biological processes involved in their expression are the only important influences in the etiology and pathogenesis of schizophrenia. We are currently engaged in analyzing these interviews with respect to experiential factors and their possible inter-action with biological vulnerability to make possible or prevent the development of schizophrenia.

References

Gottesman, I. I., and Shields, J.: *Schizophrenia and Genetics: A Twin Study Vantage Point.* New York: Academic Press, 1972.

Kety, S. S.: Biochemical theories of schizophrenia. *Science* 129: 1528-32; 1590-96, 1959.

Kety, S. S.; Rosenthal, D.; Wender, P. H.; and Schulsinger, F.: The types and prevalance of mental illness in the biological and adoptive families of adopted schizophrenics. In *The Transmission of Schizophrenia*, ed. D. Rosenthal and S. S. Kety. Oxford: Pergamon Press, 1968.

Kety, S. S.; Rosenthal, D.; Wender, P. H.; Schulsinger, F.; and Jacobsen, B.: Mental illness in the biological and adoptive families of adopted individuals who have become schizophrenic: a preliminary report based upon psychiatric interviews. In *Genetic Research in Psychiatry*, ed. R. Fieve, D. Rosenthal, and H. Brill. Baltimore: Johns Hopkins University Press, 1975.

Rosenthal, D.: Problems of sampling and diagnosis in the major twin studies of schizophrenia. *J. Psychiat. Res.* 128: 307-11, 1971.

Rosenthal, D.; Wender, P. H.; Kety, S. S.; Schulsinger, F.; Welner, J.; and Ostergaard, L.: Schizophrenics' offspring reared in adoptive homes. In *The Transmission of Schizophrenia*, ed. D. Rosenthal and S. S. Kety. Oxford: Pergamon Press, 1968.

Wender, P. H.; Rosenthal, D.; Kety, S. S.; Schulsinger, F.; and Welner, J.: Crossfostering: a research strategy for clarifying the role of genetic and experiental factors in the etiology of schizophrenia. *Arch. Gen. Psychiat.* 30: 121-28, 1974.

III

NEUROENDOCRINE STRATEGIES IN PSYCHIATRIC RESEARCH

Edward J. Sachar *

Over the past 25 years the study of brain influences on endocrine function has become a useful strategy in psychiatric research. During this period three lines of psychoendocrine investigation have been, in my view, of special interest. One is the study of the influence of psychological stress on endocrine function. A second has been the analysis of neuroendocrine regulation as a way of studying hypothalamic function in psychotic states. The most recent has been the use of hormonal responses to document the effects of psychotropic drugs on the brain.

By the early 1950s advances in endocrine biochemistry made it possible to measure sensitively in animals and man hormonal responses to stress. Drs. Mason and Brady and their colleagues at the Walter Reed Army Institute of Research demonstrated clearly in monkeys the power of pure psychological stress to alter drastically patterns of hormonal secretions, eliminating physical stress by ingenious paradigms (Mason 1968). What was initially puzzling in the human studies, however, was the generally small changes in mean corticosteroid excretion for the groups as a whole and the large variance within the groups, despite the grueling nature of the stresses. Using the Meyerian model of emphasizing adaptive processes, it proved possible to relate differences among individuals to differences in the effectiveness of their coping

*Professor and chairman/Department of Psychiatry/Columbia College of Physicians and Surgeons and Director/Department of Mental Hygiene/New York State Psychiatric Institute/New York, New York

25

and defensive mechanisms in dealing with stressful stimuli. Those able to defend themselves psychologically were found also to have protected themselves from significant corticosteroid increases. Similarly, measurement of changes in corticosteroid excretion during the course of acute schizophrenic reactions helped clarify stages of ego decompensation and recompensation during illnesses. During acute psychotic turmoil and panic states we observed huge increases in corticosteroid excretion, which subsided as patients developed organized delusional systems and became calm (Sachar et al. 1963, 1970). These delusional systems, though maladaptive in the Meyerian sense, appeared thus to serve a homeostatic function, both psychologically and physiologically.

These contributions to ego psychology, however, have tended to obscure another potential application of stress endocrinology—to psychosomatic medicine. Not only corticosteroids and adrenalin, but also prolactin, growth hormone, and testosterone have been shown to be acutely responsive to psychological stress. The widespread effects of the hormones on somatic processes, ranging from metabolism to immune responses, suggest that stress-induced hormonal changes might well influence vulnerability to medical illness or exacerbate preexisting medical pathology.

A second major thrust in psychoendocrinology has been the study of neuroendocrine function in the psychoses, particularly in the affective disorders. There are two reasons for suspecting neuroendocrine involvement in major depressive illness. First, the clinical picture suggests diffuse hypothalamic dysfunction—disturbances in mood, appetite, sexual and aggressive drives, sleep, and autonomic activity. Second, the neurotransmitters implicated in depressive illness—noradrenalin and serotonin—also play an important role in regulating the release of hypothalamic neurohormones that modulate anterior pituitary secretion.

There appear to be several neurotransmitters involved in regulating growth hormone (GH) responses, presumably through their effects on the hypothalamic factors, GH releasing factor (GHRF) and GH inhibiting factor (somatostatin). Dopamine, serotonin, noradrenalin, and their precursors are all stimulatory to GH secretion, and both serotonin and noradrenalin probably mediate the GH response to hypoglycemia, a standard clinical test for GH secretion (Martin 1976). If brain serotonin or noradrenalin (or both) is functionally depleted in depressive illness, one would expect that depressed patients would have deficient GH responses to a standard insulin-induced hypoglycemic test. We found just that, as have other laboratories. Our latest approach to this problem involved study of postmenopausal women to eliminate the variable of estrogen secretion, which potentiates GH responses

(Gruen, Sachar, and Altman 1975). We found that ten postmenopausal women suffering primary major unipolar depressive illness had significantly diminished GH responses to hypoglycemia, compared with a matched group of normal postmenopausal women.

The secretion of ACTH and cortisol is also subject to noradrenergic and serotonergic influences, but in this instance a noradrenergic system appears to inhibit ACTH secretion, while serotonin may stimulate it (Jones 1976; Van Loon 1973). Brain noradrenalin depletion stimulates cortisol secretion. Extensive research of the past two decades has established that most patients with severe depressions do markedly hypersecrete cortisol, but it has been unclear how much is a stress response related to emotional turmoil and how much is a more fundamental neuroendocrine abnormality (Sachar and Coppen 1975). With advances in psychiatric diagnosis, it is possible to separate patients with neurotic depressions from those with the pure, primary depressive illness. In the latter cases the evidence is strongly in favor of a true neuroendocrine dysfunction. Thus, hypersecretion occurs in some patients with primary "endogenous" depressions who, though markedly ill, are apathetic and emotionally flat rather than aroused (Sachar 1975). Furthermore, the cortisol hypersecretion of emotionally aroused schizophrenics is readily suppressed by dexamethasone, but the cortisol hypersecretion in depressives is relatively resistant to suppression by dexamethasone (Carroll et al. 1976). With colleagues at Albert Einstein, we explored this question of hypersecretion by studying the twenty-four-hour secretory pattern of cortisol in normal individuals and in unipolar depressed patients. We wanted to know how the extra cortisol was secreted. The normal pattern involves a series of seven to nine distinct secretory bursts, beginning about 2:00 to 3:00 A.M., synchronized with the sleep-wake cycle. Each cortisol secretory episode reflects a burst of ACTH secretion and, presumably, a pulse of hypothalamic neuroendocrine activity. Of special interest is a six-hour period in the late evening and early morning hours when cortisol secretion ceases—perhaps reflecting a central inhibition.

In contrast, the unipolar depressed patient shows a pattern of hypersecretion extending throughout the entire day, including the hours of sleep and especially during the previously mentioned quiescent period. The disturbed pattern reverts to normal after clinical recovery. When the mean twenty-four-hour pattern of several unipolar depressives is compared with the normal pattern, it appears that the major differences occur in the afternoon, evening, and early morning hours, rather than during the morning hours when cortisol is normally maximally secreted (figure 3.1) (Sachar 1975). The hypersecretion persists even during sleep. It is hard for us to reconcile these particular distortions in the twenty-four-hour curve with a simple stress hypothesis, which would predict hypersecretion primarily during waking hours and ordinarily would not specify the late evening as a period of special stress. The data might fit better with a disinhibition hypothesis, however, in which central noradrenalin depletion would result in relative hypersecretion during periods when ACTH secretion was normally inhibited.

A third psychoendocrine research strategy also holds considerably promise—the use of neuroendocrine techniques to clarify problems in neuropharmacology. A drug's effects on brain neurotransmitters may be illuminated by studying its effects on hormone systems regulated by those neurotransmitters. The first example involves studies of the effects of *d*- and *l*-amphetamine on neuroendocrine function. There is controversy in the literature about the relative effects of these two isomers on noradrenergic and dopaminergic neurons in various regions of the brain (Marantz et al. 1976). One group concluded that in the limbic system the combined noradrenergic effects of *d*-amphetamine are ten times those of *l*-amphetamine, while other groups have reported that *d*- and *l*-amphetamine are approximately equipotent in their noradrenergic effects. These studies on brain tissue actions and individual neurons left open the question of the actual net physiological action of these isomers on the intact limbic system.

Drs. Marantz, Weitzman, Sassan, and I administered equivalent doses of *d*- and *l*-amphetamine intravenously to monkeys and determined the responses of catecholaminergically regulated hormone systems, in particular cortisol and growth hormone. We found that *d*- and *l*-amphetamine equally suppressed cortisol secretion, consistent with our previous comments about a noradrenergic system inhibitory to ACTH and cortisol secretion. To show

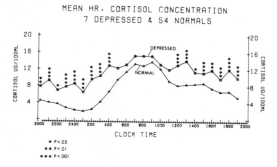

Figure 3.1. Mean twenty-four-hour pattern of hourly cortisol concentrations in seven depressed and fifty-four normal subjects.

that the hormonal responses were not caused by amphetamine's effect on dopamine, we then repeated the experiment after pretreatment of the animals with pimozide, a neuroleptic that specifically blocks dopamine receptors, leaving noradrenalin receptors untouched. The responses after pimozide were identical, and *d*- and *l*-amphetamine continued to suppress cortisol secretion equally.

Similarly, *d* and *l*-amphetamine also equally stimulated GH secretion, and blockade of dopamine receptors by pimozide did not affect the GH responses to either form of amphetamine. We concluded, then, that *d*- and *l*-amphetamine have equivalent physiological effects on noradrenergic activity in the neuroendocrine system (Marantz et al. 1976).

Recently psychopharmacologists have been studying a brain dopaminergic system—the tuberoinfundibular system—which regulates by inhibition the secretion of prolactin from the anterior pituitary (MacLeod 1976). Dopamine antagonists, such as chlorpromazine, stimulate prolactin secretion, while dopamine agonists, such as *l*-dopa, suppress prolactin secretion.

How might the psychopharmacologist make use of this tuberoinfundibular prolactin system? For one thing, he could use it to test the hypothesis that all effective antipsychotic drugs have in common the ability to block dopamine receptors or to reduce dopaminergic activity. If so, they should all stimulate prolactin secretion. My colleagues and I have studied neuroleptics of all classes—chlorpromazine, trifluoperazine, thioridazine, butaperazine, prochlorperazine, perphenazine, haloperidol, pimozide, fluphenazine, thiothexene, loxapine, molindone, etc. All stimulate prolactin secretion in humans, even thioridazine, which has little effect on the neostriatal dopamine system, which is a poor antagonist of the dopaminergic effects of apomorphine and dextroamphetamine, and which is associated clinically with few extra pyramidal side effects.

Of further interest was our finding that thiethylperazine, a paperazine phenothiazine marketed as an antiemetic, also was a potent prolactin stimulant in man. We predicted that it would prove to be an effective antischizophrenic drug, and this has subsequently been confirmed by colleagues at New York University. A possible exception to the rule that all antischizophrenic agents stimulate prolactin is clozapine. This European drug has virtually no extrapyramidal side effects and has shown weak or absent potency in blocking dopamine in most test systems. In three normal subjects who received 12.5 mg orally, we could demonstrate no prolactin elevations, although all subjects became markedly sedated.

Turning to psychotropic drugs that have no antischizophrenic properties—such as diazepam, promethazine, dephenhydramine, lithium, tricyclic antidepressants—we find that none of them stimulates prolactin in humans. It would appear, then, that the human prolactin response test would be an excellent screening test for potential antischizophrenic drugs, providing a link between animal and in vitro studies on the one hand and full-fledged clinical trials on the other.

A stricter test of the antidopamine hypothesis of the therapeutic action of neuroleptics is to demonstrate that the potency of the drugs in blocking dopamine transmission correlates with their clinical potency. Our preliminary studies suggest that the human prolactin-stimulating potencies of several neuroleptics correlate well with clinical potency. We first administered chlorpromazine 25 mg, haloperidol 1 mg, butaperazine 5 mg, and thioridazine 25 mg orally to two subjects on different occasions. We measured the increase in prolactin concentration after each dose and then, for each subject, calculated the prolactin increase in mg/ml per mg of drug administered. This figure compared to that found for chlorpromazine, as the reference drug. Using this crude approach, thioridazine was found to be approximately equipotent with chlorpromazine in stimulating prolactin, while butaperazine was eleven to nineteen times more potent and haloperidol two times more potent yet than butaperazine—quite consistent with their clinical potency. Similar results were obtained in three subjects who received IM doses of chlorpromazine, trifluoperazine, and haloperidol, which had relative prolactin-stimulating potencies of 1:12:51. Thus far, for prolactin potency, the test also seems to confirm the dopamine hypothesis in man.

Another neuropharmacologic question relates to differences between the effects of neuroleptics on the major neostriatal dopamine system, which projects to the caudate, and their effects on the hypothesized dopamine system, where the drugs exert their antischizophrenic effects. Tolerance rapidly develops to the antidopamine effects of neuroleptics in the extrapyramidal system but not to their antipsychotic effects. Anticholinergic drugs promptly reverse the extrapyramidal side effects of neuroleptics but not their antipsychotic effects. We wondered whether the tuberoinfundibular system would behave neuropharmacologically like the extrapyramidal dopamine system or more like the "therapeutic" dopamine system in these respects.

We found that tolerance did not develop in the prolactin response to sustained doses of neuroleptics over several weeks on schizophrenic subjects and that several anticholinergic drugs had no effect on plasma prolactin. Thus, in these respects, the tuberoinfundibular dopamine system behaved very much as did the "therapeutic" dopamine system and thus should be an especially useful model for the pharmacologist.

In summary, then, neuroendocrine techniques are proving of considerable value in clinical psychiatric research—in studying stress responses in relation to coping mechansims and psychosomatic phenomena, in studying brain dysfunction in the psychoses, and in analyzing the neurotransmitter effects of psychotropic drugs. It will surely not be long before still new psychoendocrine research strategies are developed.

References

Carroll, B. J.; Curtis, G. C.; and Mendels, J.: Neuroendocrine regulation in depression. *Arch. Gen. Psychiat.* 33: 1039-58, 1976.

Gruen, P. H.; Sachar, E. J.; and Altman, N.: Growth hormone response to hypoglycemia in postmenopausal depressed women. *Arch. Gen. Psychiat.* 32: 31-33, 1975.

Jones, M. T.: Secretion of corticotropin releasing hormone in vitro. In *Frontiers in Neuroendocrinology*, IV, ed. L. Martini and W. F. Ganong. New York: Raven Press, 1976.

MacLeod, R. M.: Regulation of prolactin secretions. In *Frontiers in Neuroendocrinology*, IV, ed. L. Martini and W. F. Ganong. New York: Raven Press, 1976.

Marantz, R.; Sachar, E. J.; Weitzman, E.; et al.: Cortisol and GH responses to *d*- and *l*- amphetamine in monkeys. *Endocrinology* 99: 459-65, 1976.

Martin, J.B.: Brain regulation of growth hormone secretion. In *Frontiers in Neuroendocrinology*, IV, ed. L. Martini and W. F. Ganong. New York: Raven Press, 1976.

Mason, J.: The organization of psychoendocrine mechanisms. *Psychosom. Med.* 30: 565-808, 1968.

_____ : Psychologic stress and endocrine functions. In *Topics in Psychoendocrinology*, ed. E. J. Sachar. New York: Grune and Stratton, 1975.

Sachar, E. J.: Neuroendocrine abnormalities in depressive illness. In *Topics in Psychoendocrinology*, ed. E. J. Sachar. New York: Grune and Stratton, 1975.

Sachar, E. J.: Twenty-four-hour cortisol secretory patterns in depressed and manic patients. In *Progress in Brain Research*, Vol 42, ed. W. H. Gispen et al. Amsterdam: Elsevier, 1975.

Sachar, E. J., and Coppen, A.: Biological aspects of affective psychoses. In *Biology of Brain Dysfunction*, III, ed. G. Gaull. New York: Plenum Press, 1975.

Sachar, E. J.; Mason, J.; Kolmer, H. S.; and Artiss, K.: Psychoendocrine aspects of acute schizophrenic reactions. *Psychosom. Med.* 25: 510-37, 1963.

Sachar, E. J.; Stanley, S.; Kanter, S. S.; Buie, D.; Engel, R.; and Mehlman, R.: Psychoendocrinology of ego disintegration. *Am J. Psychiat.* 126: 1067-68, 1970.

Van Loon, G. R.: Brain catecholamines and ACTH secretion. In *Frontiers in Neuroendocrinology*, ed. W. F. Ganong and L. Martini. New York: Oxford University Press, 1973.

IV

PSYCHOSOMATIC EFFECTS OF LEARNING

*Neal E. Miller**

The human ability to learn, especially to learn spoken and written language, has enabled each new generation to learn from the cumulative cultural experience of all the preceding ones. Thus it has produced an accelerated increase in our knowledge and skills. One can take progress in the field of transportation as a simple example of the contrast between the slow rate of change in the past and the recent rapid acceleration in change. From the days of the Roman Empire to the founding of our republic, there was very little if any increase in the speed of overland transportation. Indeed, during the first years of our republic, little progress was made. In the mid-nineteenth century it took about eight months for the average wagon train to cross the continent to St. Louis and then on over the Oregon Trail. But there has been a fantastically accelerating change since then. When I was a graduate student forty years ago, it took me four and a half days to get across the continent by train; now, with a favorable wind, one can get across by air in four and a half hours. But a space satellite crosses the continent overhead in about ten minutes. After almost twenty centuries of very little change the time to travel 2,500 miles shrinks from eight months to four and a half days, to four and a half hours, to ten minutes! There have been similar changes in other fields. They have freed all but the poorest people, in the developed countries, from the physical effects of predatory animals, backbreaking manual labor, hunger, cold, and the killer plagues of infectious illnesses. But the same rapidly

*Professor and Head of Laboratory of Physiological Psychology/The Rockefeller University/New York, New York

Work reported from the author's laboratory was supported by USPHS research grants MH 19991 and MH 26920.

accelerating progress that has freed us from the foregoing physical stresses is producing psychological stresses by forcing us to learn to deal with rapid technological and social changes. Thus, as the importance of infectious disease is reduced, the importance of psychosomatic effects is increased.

Epidemiological and Clinical Evidence

A number of epidemiological studies have investigated conditions that require learning to make difficult adjustments, such as immigration to a radically new environment, rapid social changes in the same environment, membership in groups with conflicting mores, membership in groups with low social status, social disorganization, and the loss of social support. These studies have shown that all such conditions can greatly increase the risk of mental disorders and of psychosomatic symptoms, such as ulcers, hypertension, myocardial infarction, and sudden cardiac death. But the interesting thing is that these conditions are also associated with considerably increased risks for other adverse medical consequences, such as tuberculosis, diabetes, leukemia, multiple sclerosis, and a wide range of minor complaints (Lowenstein 1961; Cassel 1975).

Furthermore, studies of individual cases, some of them prospective, show that the greater the number and the more drastic the changes that have occurred within the last two years of the patient's life—for example, losing a spouse, or even a favorable change, such as getting a large promotion to a better position—the greater the risk is for any one of a wide variety of mental and physical disorders (Dohrenwend and Dohrenwend 1974). They don't predict a particular disorder but do predict the risk of some undesirable consequence.

Experimental Evidence

Although ingenious controls have been used in some of these studies, it is difficult to rule out completely such factors as diet, sanitation, pollution, and health care. However, there have been a number of experimental studies, necessarily most of them on animals, that have backed up these general clinical and epidemiological conclusions. Pavlov (1927) produced severe behavioral disturbances in dogs, which he called an experimental neurosis, by subjecting them to problems that were beyond their learning ability; for example, discriminations between cues that were too similar. In poineering work, Horsley Gantt (1944) extended the range of these observations to include sexual disturbances in dogs. Gantt's dogs also showed cardiac and gastrointestinal disturbances. The really remarkable thing about these observations is that no punishment was used in these experiments. All Gantt did was to increase gradually the difficulty of the discrimination after the dog was fully engaged in the task until it became impossible. This purely psychological type of stress, not involving any physical punishment, produced these striking effects.

Role of Purely Psychological Factors in Gastric Lesions

Let us now turn to some experiments from my laboratory that bring out especially clearly the role of purely psychological factors. Figure 4.1 presents a diagram of the general idea behind these experiments. In a dangerous situation, learning affects the amount and duration of an emotion, such as fear, which via innate physiological processes produces the end result of stomach lesions. Instead of the general concept of stress, I shall refer more specifically during these experiments to fear, or anxiety as it is called when its source is vague or ubiquitous.

The kind of situation in which a purely psychological factor was isolated is illustrated in Figure 4.2. Three rats are restrained in separate soundproof compartments, the walls of which are not shown. Each rat has a fixed electrode on its tail. For the first two rats these electrodes are wired in series so that they get exactly the same strength of electric shock. The lucky control rat has the same electrode but gets no shock. The only difference between the first two is that one of them has a signal so that he can learn to discriminate when it is dangerous and when it is safe, and the other one receives the same signal but at a different time so that it is not correlated with the shock and he cannot learn to discriminate when it is dangerous and when it is safe. This general type of design was first used in my laboratory by Dr. Arlo Myers (1956). He measured fear by its inhibitory effect on drinking when the rat was thirsty, and he found that the animal that had the cue that enabled it to discriminate showed much less generalized fear of the situation than the other rat.

Figure 4.1. Diagram illustrating the effect of learning on the strength of an emotion such as fear, which in turn has an innate tendency to produce the psychosomatic effect of stomach lesions. L—learning; I—innate chain of events.

Later, Dr. Jay Weiss (1970) in my laboratory secured the results shown in Figure 4.3. From mere loose restraint without food, the nonshocked control group had very few stomach lesions. The group with the signaled shock, which could learn the discriminations, had somewhat more stomach lesions. The group with the unsignaled shock had five times more extensive stomach lesions than their partners who received signaled shock. So you can see that, in exposure to exactly the same strength of physical stressor, electric shock, the purely psychological variable of having a cue that allowed the rats to learn to discriminate when it was dangerous and when it was safe made a large difference in the physical effects of fear as shown by stomach lesions. Dollard and Miller (1950) have emphasized the value of learning such a discrimination during psychotherapy.

Figure 4.4 shows another situation devised by Weiss (1971a) in which the tails of the first two rats are wired in series so that they get exactly the same

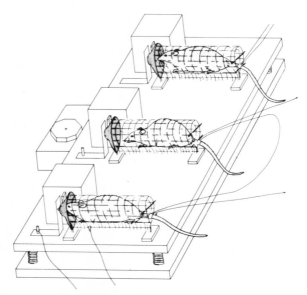

Figure 4.2. Apparatus for studying the effect of being able to learn a discrimination on the strength of fear and on stomach lesions. The rats are semirestrained in separate soundproof compartments. The first two rats receive exactly the same strength of electric shock because the electrodes on their tails are wired in series. The electrode on the third (control) rate is not connected to any source of shock. The first rat receives a tone as a signal predicting the shock; the second one receives the same tone uncorrelated with shock.

Source: J. M. Weiss, Effects of coping responses on stress, *J. Comp. Physiol. Psychol.* 65: 251-60, 1968.

electric shocks. The first rat can perform a coping response—turning a wheel—that will control the shock. If he turns the wheel promptly enough, he will avoid the shock; if not, he cannot escape it. A second, yoked-control, rat has access to the same type of wheel, but his wheel is not connected to anything so that he is at the mercy of his stupid partner. The third rat is the one who gets no shocks. Figure 4.5 shows the results. You can see that the avoidance group, who had the simple coping response of turning the wheel, developed only somewhat more lesions than the group not getting any shocks. But the yoked group, which were at the mercy of their stupid partners, got far more stomach lesions. So we see here the effect of a second psychological factor, the chance to learn to perform a coping response. Adolf Meyer has emphasized the importance of coping responses in managing human stresses, as have Dollard and Miller (1950).

In the foregoing experiment the rats who performed the coping response had fewer stomach lesions than those who could not. This result is the opposite of that in the experiment in which Brady et al. (1958) showed that the so-called executive monkeys had more extensive ulcers than their yoked controls. You might say that this is a species difference: that it is easy to be an executive provided you are a rat. But we didn't think that; we thought it was a function of the nature of the task. Figure 4.6 shows the results of an experiment by Weiss (1971b) on this point. The left side shows results of a repetition of the earlier experiment in which the animals that could perform a simple coping response had fewer stomach lesions. The right side shows

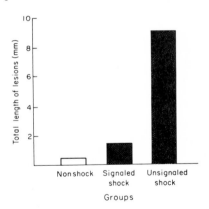

Figure 4.3. The effect of being able to learn a discrimination on the number of stomach lesions produced by electric shocks of equal physical intensity. The group with signaled shock can learn the discrimination; the one with unsignaled shock cannot.

Source: Data from J. M. Weiss, Somatic effects of predictable and unpredictable shock, *Psychosom. Med.* 32: 397-408, 1970.

results in a situation that produces a lot of conflict, where the avoidance (executive) rat has to take a shock in order to turn off a longer train of shocks. His yoked partner gets exactly the same shocks, but you can see the comparison between the two groups is reversed: the avoidance group has far more stomach lesions than the yoked one. Apparently, in a simple situation it is a great advantage to be in an executive position, but in a conflict-inducing one it can be a great disadvantage. The fact that one can get such a strong interaction with the same variable producing opposite effects in different situations means that one should be cautious of my explanation; we need more experiments to isolate exactly what the nature of the various interacting factors are. Again, that experiment shows the importance of a purely psychological factor, presumably the factor of conflict.

Effects on Corticosterone and Norepinephrine

In all of the preceding experiments the treatments that produced the greater amounts of stomach lesions also produced higher levels of plasma

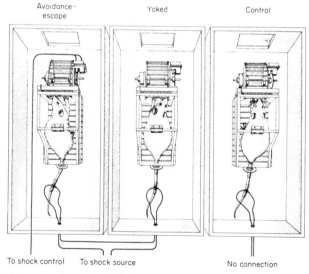

Figure 4.4. Apparatus for studying the effects of being able to learn an avoidance coping response. The rats are in separate soundproof compartments. The first rat can avoid or escape the electric shock by rotating the wheel. The second, yoked, rat receives exactly the same shocks because electrodes on the tails of the two animals are wired in series, but his wheel is not connected to the shock-control apparatus.

Source: Adapted from J. M. Weiss, Psychological factors in stress and disease, *Sci. Amer.* 226, 6: 104-13, 1972.

corticosterone. Furthermore, within each treatment the rats with higher levels of plasma corticosterone tended to have more stomach lesions.

Returning to the situation in which the avoidance response was a simple, clear-cut one that did not induce conflict, Figure 4.7 shows that, when compared with control rats, those who could perform the simple coping response had higher levels of norepinephrine in the brain whereas their helpless, yoked partners had lower levels. Two other experiments, one of which controlled for amount of physical activity, have confirmed this general result (Weiss, Glazer, and Pohorecky 1976). As has been shown, the drugs that are useful in treating a depression are those that produce an increase in the effectiveness of norepinephrine and possibly other monoamines in the synapse and that the drugs that have the opposite effect of causing or intensifying depression are those that have the opposite effect of depleting norepinephrine and other monoamines. Schildkraut (1969) has advanced the hypothesis that situationally induced depressions may involve the same reduction in effectiveness of norepinephrine at the synapse. The experiments that have just been described provide evidence that a hopeless situation does indeed produce a reduction in norepinephrine. Perhaps this is a normal mechanism for producing a depressed mood, which may be adaptive in preventing an animal from wasting too much energy by struggling with a hopeless situation. But perhaps when this mechanism is brought into play too strongly by either a biochemical error or an extraordinarily hopeless

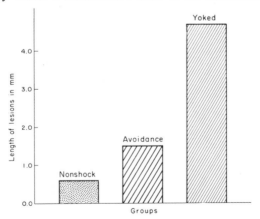

Figure 4.5. The effect of being able to perform a coping response on the length of stomach lesions. Each yoked rat receives exactly the same electric shocks as his avoidance partner because the electrodes on their tails are wired in series.

Source: Data from J. M. Weiss, Effects of coping responses on stress, *J. Comp. Physiol. Psychol.* 65: 251-60, 1968.

situation, it may lead to a maladaptively low level, which in turn may create further failure, thus producing a vicious circle of reduced norepinephrine and continued depression. Conversely, the increased level of norepinephrine in the animals that can perform a coping response may be a normal means for producing an elevation in mood that helps to energize successful responses. One might even speculate that this increased level of norepinephrine suggests a positive mental-health value for meeting and successfully overcoming difficulties.

Brain Amines and Behavioral Aftereffects of Stress

The vicious-circle hypothesis just decribed assumes that a stress-induced depletion in norepinephrine will have a depressive effect on behavior. In order to secure evidence on this point, a series of experiments was performed in which some rats were subjected to the severe stress of swimming in cold water and others to that of unpredictable, inescapable electric shocks. These treatments were indeed found to reduce the level of norepinephrine in the brain (Glazer et al. 1975) and to produce a transient depression in the ability of the rats to learn and perform a shuttle-avoidance response in a situation involving the effort of crossing a barrier (Weiss and Glazer 1975). This was not a general interference with learning, since the rats could learn a much less effortful avoidance response. In the more effortful situation involving the

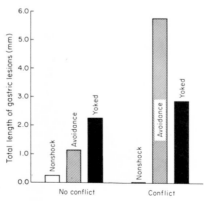

Figure 4.6. Being the "executive" rat that learns the avoidance task reduces the length of stomach lesions when the task is simple and clear-cut but increases it when the task involves conflict. In each case, the avoidance and yoked rats receive exactly the same shocks because electrodes on their tails are wired in series.

Source: J. M. Weiss, Effects of punishing the coping response (conflict) on stress pathology in rats, *J. Comp. Physiol. Psychol.* 77: 14-21, 1971.

barrier, the rats were physically able to perform this response but did not seem able to muster the psychological activation to attempt it. The fact that this behavioral deficiency could be prevented by pargyline, a drug that helps to counteract the depletion of norepinephrine and other monoamines, and could be very closely mimicked by the effects of an injection of tetrabenazine, a drug that has the opposite effect of depleting these amines, yielded further evidence that the depletion of these amines was indeed a cause of the behavioral depression.

Neither of the foregoing two effects of drugs would be expected from the learned-helplessness hypothesis advanced by Overmeir and Seligman (1967) and by Seligman and Maier (1967). Thus, that hypothesis does not appear to apply to the behavior observed in this particular experimental situation. On the other hand, that something like learned helplessness or its opposite, learned resourcefulness, can indeed occur under suitable circumstances has been discussed theoretically by Dollard and Miller (1950, pp. 132-33). Furthermore, learned resistance to pain and fear has been demonstrated experimentally by Miller (1960) and by Feirstein and Miller (1963).

Brain Amines and Habituation to Stress

One might expect unlearned as well as learned factors to be involved in the development of behavioral resistance to stress. Depletion of the neuro-

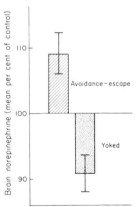

Figure 4.7. Compared with nonshock (control) rats, those that are able to perform an avoidance-escape response have an increased level of norepinephrine in their brains, their helpless yoked partners, who have no coping response available, have a decreased level of norepinephrine.

Source: J. M. Weiss, E. A. Stone, and N. Harrell, Coping behavior and brain norepinephrine level in rats, *J. Comp. Physiol. Psychol.* 72: 153-60, 1970.

transmitters, such as norepinephrine, removes the process of synthesis from inhibition by its end product and thus induces an increase in the activity of the enzyme, tyrosine hydroxylase, that synthesizes it. From this phenomenon we might expect that rats exposed to strong inescapable shocks on each day for a number of days would increase their capacity to synthesize norepinephrine and hence would suffer less depletion after one of the later exposures. Then, if the depletion is indeed the primary factor in the behavioral deficit, they should show less of such a deficit.

Experiments were performed to test this hypothesis (Weiss et al. 1975). Rats that were exposed to severe shocks each day for fifteen days showed a higher level of activity in the enzyme tyrosine hydroxylase, which synthesizes norepinephrine, than did rats that received the shocks for the first time on the fifteenth day. As would be expected from this increased synthesis, the previously exposed rats showed much less depletion of norepinephrine than those that had not previously been toughened up. As an unexpected result, the rats that had previous exposures showed also a lower rate of reuptake of norepinephrine than those that had not. Both this reduction in reuptake and the lessened depletion would be expected to have the same effect of making norepinephrine more effective at the synapse, which in turn should make the behavior of the previously exposed rats more normal than that of the ones being shocked for the first time. Behavioral tests bore out this prediction.

In addition, the previous habituation to shock also considerably reduced the degree to which the test shocks elevated the level of plasma corticosterone.

Finally, if the foregoing beneficial effects of prior habituation to electric shocks are indeed a function of a depletion of norepinephrine (and possibly of other monoamines) rather than of some other more general effects of the daily stress, exposing the animal to fourteen prior drug-induced drug depletions should have similar beneficial effects on its behavior after severe shocks. Glazer et al. (1975) tested this prediction by using tetrabenazine, a drug that produces a rapid but transient depletion in norepinephrine and also in other monoamines. Figure 4.8 shows that this prediction was confirmed. The animals that had the placebo treatment throughout—i.e., fourteen days of isotonic saline placebo injections as a pretreatment and a fifteenth such placebo injection immediately before their test in the shuttle avoidance apparatus—showed good performance in that test, as indicated by low latencies that become progressively lower during training, thus showing that they learned. The animals that had placebo pretreatment and received either inescapable shocks in a different apparatus or an injection of tetrabenazine immediately before the test showed poor performance, as indicated by long latencies and failure to improve during training. These results confirmed those of the earlier experiments on the effects of severe inescapable shocks and of an amine-depleting drug on learning and performance. In contrast with the above two groups, it can be seen that the rats that received tetrabenazine pretreatments were protected from the disrupting effects of tetrabenazine immediately before the test and were also protected from the effects of the strong inescapable shocks immediately before the test; these two groups were no different from the group that received placebo throughout.

The results of the foregoing series of experiments show that either a prior habituation to the stress of strong inescapable shocks or a prior habituation to a tetrabenazine-induced depletion of norepinephrine and other monoamines can protect rats from the behavioral disruption produced by subsequent exposure to the stress of severe unpredictable, inescapable electric shocks.

It seems highly probable that the temporal distribution of the trials for habituation to stress will be found to be a critical factor. If these trials are too widely spaced, the habituating effects may be dissipated; if they are too closely spaced, the effects of the successive depletions may combine to produce a greater depletion instead of a resistance to depleting effects.

Both the unlearned and the learned effects of prior exposure to stress merit further investigation. I am reminded of the pioneering work of Curt Richter (1957), who showed that if you cut off the whiskers of wild rats,

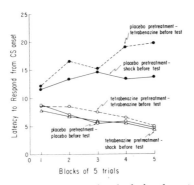

Figure 4.8. Prior exposure to a norepinephrine-depleting drug, tetrabenazine, "toughens up" the rats so that they are able to learn the avoidance task immediately after exposure either to that drug or to traumatic electric shocks in a different apparatus.

Source: H. I. Glazer et al., Monoamines as mediators of avoidance-escaping behavior, *Psychosom. Med.* 37: 535-43, 1975.

which apparently makes them feel especially helpless, and put them in a situation where they have to swim with jets of water bearing down on them, many of them will suddenly die after a short exposure. But if you give these rats a chance to escape just once from this situation, when you later expose them again they will keep swimming for a long, long time.

Effects on Cardiovascular and Immune Systems

There are a number of experiments indicating that stress can induce or aggravate hypertension in some animals that are especially susceptible, because of either a genetic or an organically induced predisposing factor (Shapiro and Melhado 1957; Friedman and Dahl 1975). Furthermore, stress induced by electric shock seems to potentiate the adverse cardiovascular effects of diets high in cholesterol or saturated fats (Rothfield et al. 1973; Cairncross and Bassett 1975). Lown, Verrier, and Corbalan (1973) have found that the threshold for producing an arrhythmia just one step short of fatal fibrillation is reduced by testing dogs in a room where they had previously been exposed to electric shocks instead of testing them in a room where they had received good treatment.

A series of experimental studies has shown that a variety of stressful interventions, such as chronic exposure to avoidance learning, can reduce an animal's resistance to a variety of experimental infections (Rasmussen, Marsh, and Brill 1957; Johnson et al. 1963; Johnson and Rasmussen 1965; Friedman, Glasgow, and Ader 1969; Rasmussen 1969). Other studies show increased tolerance to a skin graft (Wistar and Hildemann 1960) and decreased survival time to implanted tumors (Ader and Friedman 1965) and leukemia (Levine and Cohen 1959). These studies suggest that stress can affect the immune system. A few studies have shown more direct effects on the immune system (Rasmussen, Spence, and Marsh 1959; Vessey 1964; Hill, Greer, and Felsenfeld 1967), and some studies have started to analyze the mechanisms involved—for example, by investigating the effects of adrenalectomy (Yamada, Jensen, and Rasmussen 1964). Finally, some studies finding an opposite effect—e.g., increased resistance to an experimental infection after stress (Marsh et al. 1963)—suggest the desirability of quantitative studies to look into the possibility of rebound phenomena or an inverted J-shaped function. Some of the newer and more powerful techniques for measuring various aspects of the immune system directly and following the temporal course with nondestructive tests on individual animals should be useful in such studies. Because of the importance of the immune system in such a wide range of medically significant conditions, quantitative and analytical studies of how it is affected by stress should yield significant results.

A More Powerful Experimental Design

All the experimental studies that we have described have determined the effect of one or more treatments on a single outcome—either a gastric lesion, a cardiovascular effect, or an index of a presumed effect on the immune system. In order to determine whether stress functions as a single unitary variable—different results in different individuals being determined by the different susceptibilities of different organ systems—or whether there are different types of stresses (or other psychological variables) that predispose toward different outcomes, a new type of experimental design is needed. Instead of being limited to the measurement of a single psychosomatic consequence, each experiment should involve the measurement of two or more such consequences on each individual animal. Then the effects of a number of different interventions on each of these consequences should be compared. For example, will the procedure that produces the most gastric lesions also produce the greatest cardiovascular effects, or will one kind of stressful intervention predispose toward gastrointestinal while another predisposes toward cardiovascular effects? The advantage of this type of design has been discussed elsewhere (Miller 1959, pp. 276-80; 1967; 1972a, pp. 346-47).

Effects of Instrumental Learning on Visceral Responses

Thus far, the experiments described have followed the paradigm illustrated in Figure 4.1; the effects of learning have been to change the strength and duration of fear, which in turn has produced psychosomatic effects via presumably innate mechanisms. In many cases the effects of learning were confounded with those of the painful electric shocks used to produce the learning; but in others, notably those by Weiss and Lown, the effects of learning were clearly isolated. Can learning enter the picture at another point? Figure 4.9 illustrates diagrammatically the possibility that learning can determine the direction and magnitude of the psychosomatic effect produced by a given strength of an emotion such as fear.

In classical conditioning, it is known that the nature of the conditioned response is determined by the nature of the response to the unconditioned stimulus, although, as we shall see later, there are some interesting exceptions to this rule. Thus, food that elicits the unconditioned response of salivation can be used to condition this response to a new stimulus (such as a bell), and nitroglycerine, which elicits tachycardia, can be used to establish it as a conditioned response (Bykov 1957). But can a reward or, as psychiastrists call it, a secondary gain (such as a reduction in anxiety) that does not in itself elicit a specific visceral response be used to reinforce any one of a number of visceral responses? This kind of learning is called by a variety of names: trial-and-error learning, instrumental learning, or operant conditioning. In classical conditioning, food can be used only to condition an increase in salivation and other responses that are invariably elicited by food; in trial-and-error learning, the same food can be used as a reinforcement (also called a reward) to train a dog to come when called, to sit up, to roll over, or to lie down. Furthermore, the different reward of water to a thirsty dog can be used to train the same responses. Therefore, it can be seen that this type of learning is much more flexible than classical conditioning. Can it be used to affect visceral responses? The traditional answer has been no, but recent work has questioned this view.

In the earliest clear-cut animal experiment, Miller and Carmona (1967) used water to reward changes in the salivation of thirsty dogs. Initially the water had no effect on the salivation, each tiny drop of which was separately recorded. For one group of dogs whenever there was a spontaneous burst of salivation so that the drops came more closely together, water was automatically delivered. As the dogs gradually learned to produce more and larger bursts of salivation, the amount required for reward was progressively in-

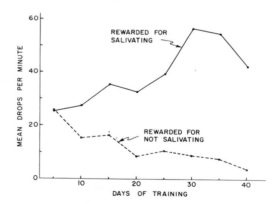

Figure 4.9. Instrumental learning of increased salivation by dogs rewarded for salivating and of decreased salivation by dogs rewarded for not salivating. Motivation is thirst, and reward is water.

Source: N. E. Miller and A. Carmona, Modification of a visceral response, salivation in thirsty dogs, by instrumental training with water reward, *J. Comp. Physiol. Psychol.* 63: 1-6, 1967.

creased. For another group the opposite response of not salivating was re-warded. As the animals learned, progressively longer intervals between drops were required to produce the reward. As Figure 4.9 shows, the rewards for opposite types of response produced them. The fact that one group learned to increase and the other group learned to decrease rules out any possible conditioned or unlearned effect of the water on the rate of salivation. Similar instrumental learning of salivation has recently been confirmed by Shapiro and Herendeen (1975), who have shown that food may be used to reward a decrease in salivation—a change in direction opposite to what would be expected from classical conditioning. Benson et al. (1969) used escape from and avoidance of electric shock to train squirrel monkeys first to increase and later to decrease their average arterial blood pressure. Engel and Gottlieb (1970) used escape from and avoidance of electric shock to train rhesus monkeys to speed up their heart rate during certain sessions and slow it down during others. In each of these cases the animals were given forty days or more of training and showed sizable changes. The fact that the changes could be obtained in either direction rules out any simple explanation in terms of classical conditioning. Harris et al. (1973) have used a combination of shock avoidance and food reward to teach baboons, during forty days of training, to produce 30-mm Hg elevations of blood pressure and to maintain them for the entire twelve-hour period of the sessions. Other baboons that were sub-jected to similar procedures, except that the reward was for decreasing blood pressure, showed neither increases nor decreases from the same shocks and rewards, so that there was a large difference between the two groups.

In the meantime a rapidly growing body of evidence, summarized by Kimmel (1974), has shown that human subjects can learn instrumentally to control in one way or another a considerable variety of visceral responses. Some of the potentially most impressive evidence is that demonstrating the specificity of such learning. For example, Shapiro, Tursky, and Schwartz (1970) have trained subjects to increase or decrease their blood pressure, respectively, without changing their heart rate and other subjects to increase or decrease their heart rate, respectively, without changing their blood pres-sure.

Other studies have been on patients suffering from cardiovascular dis-orders. For example, Engel and Bleecker (1974) have secured evidence that certain patients with premature ventricular contractions can be taught volun-tary control over such contractions, as demonstrated by the fact that after training they can turn them off or on upon request. Such specific voluntary control seems unlikely to be a nonspecific placebo effect. Pickering and Miller (1977) have confirmed these results with two additional patients. Although these results and additional ones on other cardiac arrhythmias suggest that such training may have therapeutic value, such value has not yet been definitely proved (Miller 1975).

Attempts specifically to train hypertensive patients to lower their blood pressure have produced results that to date are of marginal therapeutic magnitude and are roughly comparable with those of other behavioral approaches, such as training in increased skin resistance (presumably indicating reduced sympathetic activity), training in muscular relaxation, autogenic training, hypnosis, and meditation (Shapiro et al. 1977). In general, the alleged improvement in these cases has not been accompanied by evidence for clear-cut voluntary control, although one unusual patient (Miller 1972b) has learned to be able to change her diastolic blood pressure promptly upon request over a range of approximately 30 mm Hg.

Evaluation of Biofeedback

In the animal experiments I have just described special instrumentation was used to produce a moment-to-moment measurement of the visceral response in question. Then slight deviations in the correct direction were immediately rewarded, and the animal was shaped by progressively requiring larger changes to achieve the reward. In the human experiments the same kind of strategy was used—except that the reward was usually a digital signal, such as a tone that informed the subject he had achieved a criterion level of response, or an analog signal, such as the needle on a meter that varied with his response. In these cases the knowledge of results or, in other words, knowledge that he was succeeding, served as the reward. Such knowledge of results has been called feedback, and feedback concerning a biological function has been called biofeedback. Theoretically, we would expect it to be most helpful in cases in which the response is learnable but the natural feedback is poorly or incorrectly perceived. Most people have poor perception of their visceral responses, and some even have poor perception of certain types of chronic muscular tension. Some patients being rehabilitated from severe accidents or strokes apparently have poor perception of the feedback from certain responses, such as whether they have locked their knee when they are trying to stand or walk.

As with many new developments, the use of biofeedback to extend the domain of learning to new kinds of responses has caught the public fancy so that its current therapeutic usefulness has been grossly exaggerated in the public media. There is a great danger that these exaggerations are producing impossible expectations, which will lead to inevitable disillusionment that will hamper the hard work necessary to determine what, if anything, of therapeutic value can be gained from this type of procedure.

I have summarized elsewhere the current status of therapeutic applications of biofeedback (Miller 1975, 1976; Miller and Dworkin 1977a) and the need to consider with certain patients the secondary gains that they may get from certain symptoms (Miller and Dworkin 1977b). With respect to a number of conditions—cardiac arrhythmias, hypertension, Raynaud's disease, ruminative vomiting, anal incontinence, emotional diarrhea, bruxism, headaches, epilepsy, and neuromuscular rehabilitation—initial results have been promising enough to merit further investigation with the necessary more rigorous controls for placebo effects, for regression to the mean, and for the natural tendency of the body to heal itself. In none of these applications has therapeutic value definitely been established by strict criteria.

Unpredictable Course of Scientific Research

I shall conclude this paper with some experiences in our laboratory that illustrate the unpredictable course of scientific research—something that the general public and its legislators need to be educated to understand far better than they do now. Incidentally, a book by Dr. Judith Swazey (1974) illustrates this unpredictable course very well for the series of developments that led to the therapeutic use of the drug chlorpromazine, which has largely led to the humane disappearance of the horrible stenches, shrieks, highly disruptive acts, and stark hopelessness that used to characterize the disturbed wards of mental hospitals.

To return to my own research, there are a number of ways in which instrumental learning can affect visceral responses (Miller 1976; Miller and Dworkin 1977a and b). Some of these are indirect, via the skeletal muscles, as when hyperventilation can be a cause of chronic tachycardia or when a sudden deep breath can have the therapeutic effect of interrupting certain types of paroxysmal tachycardia. In an attempt to eliminate some of these indirect ways, my colleagues and I have performed a number of experiments on rats paralyzed by curare, a drug that paralyzes the skeletal muscles but leaves the autonomic nervous system relatively unaffected (Miller 1969). At that time the procedure of paralysis seemed to facilitate greatly the learning of a variety of highly specific visceral responses. We decided that the rationale for this strong effect was that the paralysis eliminated interference and distraction by skeletal responses. These results were repeated in several other laboratories, but over a period of years the magnitude of the learned visceral changes progressively declined until neither we nor the other investigators are able to repeat the earlier results (Miller and Dworkin 1974).

Before we discovered these difficulties, we looked around for a human analogue of rats paralyzed by curare and decided that a good place to begin was with patients extensively paralyzed by polio or muscular dystrophy, conditions that paralyze the skeletal muscles but leave the visceral responses controlled by the autonomic nervous system relatively unaffected. With the administrative support of Dr. Mathew Lee, director of rehabilitation medicine at Goldwater Memorial Hospital, and the collaboration of Bernard Brucker there, we secured access to such patients and trained them to increase or decrease their blood pressure (Pickering et al. 1977). These patients did show some learned control over blood pressure, and we were able to use the specificity of this learning, which did not involve changes in heart rate, plus the paralysis and certain other control procedures to make it seem unlikely that their learned voluntary control over blood pressure was achieved indirectly via the use of the skeletal muscles. But the changes were relatively small, so we were disappointed in our original and apparently rationally well-grounded hope that the paralysis of these patients would greatly facilitate their visceral learning.

At this point an unexpected chance factor entered the scene. There was a patient at Goldwater who was paralyzed by a gunshot wound that had severed his spinal cord at T4—approximately the middle of his chest. He had powerful arms and shoulders and a great ambition to learn to walk with crutches and braces, but every time he was helped into an upright position his blood pressure fell and he fainted. After approximately two years of persistent effort, physical therapy department had given up on him. When he heard about our work on this topic, he begged Mr. Brucker to teach him

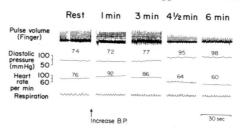

Figure 4.10. Performance of learned increase in blood pressure by patient with spinal cord severed at T4. The figures above each tracing show the blood pressure or heart rate scores, respectively, automatically integrated during each thirty-second test period. (The patient was trained by Bernard Brucker at Goldwater Memorial Hospital and recorded by Dr. Thomas Pickering in the author's laboratory.)

to increase his blood pressure. To everyone's surprise, he showed a remarkable talent for learning to increase his blood pressure. Soon his increases were so large that he could perceive them and start practicing by himself without a special apparatus to provide feedback. Figure 4.10 shows a record of a typical voluntary increase in diastolic blood pressure after training. He starts out with an initial diastolic blood pressure integrated over a 30-second period of 74 mm Hg. When asked to increase, his pressure first drops to 72 while his heart rate goes up from 76 to 92 beats per minute. After this his blood pressure starts to increase, going up to 77, 95, and eventually 98, an increase of 24 mm Hg. Meanwhile, his heart rate falls to a final level of 60 beats per minute, presumably as a result of the sino-cardiac reflex elicited by the increase in pressure. At the same time the volume of his finger pulse markedly decreases, indicating vasoconstriction that presumably is one of the means of increasing blood pressure.

The therapeutic outcome of this training is illustrated in Figure 4.11. The patient starts out with a systolic pressure of 110 mm Hg while sitting. When he is not attempting voluntary control over his blood pressure, within two minutes of his being helped into a standing position it has fallen to the low level of 50 mm Hg, at which point he is about to faint so that he has to be returned to the sitting position. But if, while sitting, he attempts to raise his blood pressure, he is able to increase it by more than 30 mm Hg and, when helped into a standing position, to maintain it at over 100 for the first two minutes or, in other words, more than 50 mm Hg above what it was when he was not attempting to keep it raised while standing. At the end of 5 minutes of standing his systolic blood pressure is still at the satisfactory level of 90

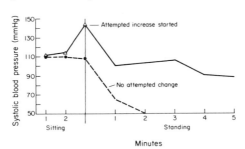

Figure 4.11. Learned voluntary increase in blood pressure counteracts the postural hypotension produced by changing patient with lesion at T4 from a sitting to a standing position. When systolic blood pressure fell to 50 mm Hg, patient was returned to sitting position.

Source: B. S. Brucker and L. P. Ince, Biofeedback as an experimental treatment for postural hypotension in a spinal cord lesioned patient, *Arch. Phys. Med. Rehab.* 1977 (in press).

mm Hg. With the aid of this voluntary control over his blood pressure, he was able to stave off fainting and learn to walk with crutches and braces. At first he would occasionally feel his blood pressure falling and have to stop walking to concentrate on raising it again, but eventually his blood pressure remained up with a minumum of conscious effort (Brucker and Ince 1977).

Brucker has studied a total of eleven patients with spinal lesions, ten of whom have shown unusual abilities to increase their blood pressure. Of these, two patients with cords severed in the neck between C4 and C5 had suffered for more than two years from postural hypotension severe enough that they could not lower their feet to a normal sitting position. For them, the training had the definite therapeutic effect of enabling them to sit in a normal position without fainting. Since the other patients did not suffer from severe postural hypotension, their training had no appreciable therapeutic effect. Pickering has studied three additional patients with high cervical transections and found that two of them had unusual ability to learn large increases in blood pressure (Pickering et al. 1977).

In the foregoing experiments various controls ruled out respiration and made it seem highly improbably that commands to intact or paralyzed muscles could be the basis for the large increases observed. The increases seemed to be due, at least partially, to a speed-up in heart rate, presumably produced by a decrement in the inhibitory activity of the vagus on the heart, since similar increases could be produced by atropine (Pickering et al. 1977). Apparently the lesion interfered with the mechanism whereby increases in heart rate are compensated for by decreases in stroke volume. But such an explanation alone cannot account for the instances (e.g., fig. 4.10) in which the blood pressure continued to go up even after the heart rate started to slow down.

Since patients with these spinal lesions have unusually large spontaneous fluctuations in blood pressure, it seems reasonable to suppose that the lesions have in some way reduced the tight homeostatic control over the level of this pressure and that this loosened control is the basis for their ability to learn unusually large increases. If a drug could be found that had a similar anti-homeostatic effect, it might be extremely useful in animal experiments on visceral learning and conceivably even in the initial stages of training human patients to achieve therapeutic effects.

Possible Role of Learning in Normal Homeostasis

Previous work on visceral learning has raised the possibility that such learning may play a hitherto unsuspected role in normal homeostasis (Miller,

Dicara, and Wolf 1968; Miller 1969). Those patients with spinal lesions who have just been described as suffering from extreme postural hypotension were able to learn to correct the abnormally low levels of blood pressure produced by a more vertical posture; their learned responses helped to restore blood pressure to a more normal homeostatic level and hence to avoid fainting. How often does learning help to achieve similar corrections?

Some of the patients with high cervical lesions who no longer suffered from severe postural hypotension reported that at first they would faint whenever their legs were lowered to a normal sitting position. But they reported having the nurse lower their legs as low as possible and fighting off the tendency to faint. In this way they overcame the postural hypotension. It seems reasonable to assume that they may actually have learned in a way similar to that of the patients who received specific training, except that in their case the variations in the perception of feeling faint provided them with the same information about changes in blood pressure that our instrumentation provided for the patients who received the specific training. How many other patients learn to overcome various visceral aberrations, either consciously or unconsciously, in a similar way? What role does visceral learning play in helping normal subjects to maintain better homeostasis or to adjust the priorities among competing homeostatic demands?

We have already mentioned the instances in which the conditioned response is opposite to the unconditioned one. Such an outcome is contrary to what would be predicted from the traditional substitution theories of classical conditioning. Yet such an outcome counteracts the deviation from a normal homeostatic level produced by the response to the unconditioned stimulus. A return to a normal homeostatic level is known to serve as a reinforcement for the learning of many skeletal responses. Could such a return serve to reinforce the learning of the visceral responses that produced it? These questions deserve further investigation; Dr. Barry Dworkin and I are beginning to work on some of them.

References

Ader, R., and Friedman, S. B.: Differential early experiences and susceptibility to transplanted tumor in the rat. *J. Comp. Physiol. Psychol.* 59: 361-64, 1965.

Benson, H.; Herd, A. J.; Morse, W. H.; and Kelleher, R. T.: Behavioral induction of arterial hypertension and its reversal. *Amer. J. Physiol.* 217: 30-34, 1969.

Brady, J. V.; Porter, R. W.; Conrad, D. G.; and Mason, J. W.: Avoidance behavior and the development of gastroduodenal ulcers. *J. Exp. Anal. Behav.* 1: 69-72, 1958.

Brucker, B. S., and Ince, L. P.: Biofeedback as an experimental treatment for postural hypotension in a spinal cord lesioned patient. *Arch. Phys. Med. Rehab.*, 1977 in press.

Bykov, K. M.: *The Cerebral Cortex and the Internal Organs.* Translated and edited by W. H. Gantt. New York: Chemical Publishing, 1957.

Cairncross, K. D., and Bassett, J. R.: Changes in myocardial function as a consequence of prolonged emotional stress. In *Hormones, Homeostasis, and the Brain*, ed. W. H. Gispen, Tj. B. van Wimersma Greidanus, B. Bohus, and D. de Wied. Amsterdam: Elsevier, 1975.

Cassel, J.: Social science in epidemiology: psychological processes and stress, theoretical formulation. In *Handbook of Evaluation Research*, ed. E. Savening and M. Guttentag. Beverly Hills, Cal.: Sage, 1975.

Dohronwend, B. S., and Dohrenwend, B. P., eds.: *Stressful Life Events.* New York: Wiley, 1974.

Dollard, J., and Miller, N. E.: *Personality and Psychotherapy.* New York: McGraw-Hill, 1950.

Engel, B. T., and Bleecker, E. R.: Application of operant conditioning techniques to the control of the cardiac arrhythmias. In *Cardiovascular Psychophysiology*, ed. P. A. Obrist, A. H. Black, J. Brener, and L. V. DiCara. Chicago: Aldine, 1974.

Engel, B. T., and Gottlieb, S. H.: Differential operant conditioning of heart rate in the restrained monkey. *J. Comp. Physiol. Psychol.* 73: 217-25, 1970.

Feirstein, A. R., and Miller, N. E.: Learning to resist pain and fear: effects of electric shock before versus after reaching goal. *J. Comp. Physiol. Psychol.* 56: 797-800, 1963.

Friedman, R., and Dahl, K.: The effect of chronic conflict on the blood pressure of rats with a genetic susceptibility to experimental hypertension. *Psychosom. Med.* 37: 402-16, 1975.

Friedman, S. B.; Glasgow, L. A.; and Ader, R.: Psychosocial factors modifying host resistance to experimental infections. *Ann. N. Y. Acad. Sci.* 164: 381-93, 1969.

Gantt, W. H.: *Experimental Basis for Neurotic Behavior.* New York: Hoeber, 1944.

Glazer, H. I.; Weiss, J. M.; Phorecky, L. A.; and Miller, N. E.: Monoamines as mediators of avoidance-escape behavior. *Psychosom. Med.* 37: 535-43, 1975.

Harris, A. J.; Gilliam, W. J.; Findley, J. D.; and Brady, J. V.: Instrumental conditioning of large-magnitude, daily, 12-hour blood pressure elevations in the baboon. *Science* 182: 175-77, 1973.

Hill, C. W.; Greer, W. E.; and Felsenfeld, D.: Psychological stress, early response to foreign protein, and blood cortisol in vervets. *Psychosom. Med.* 29: 279-83, 1967.

Johnson, T.; Lavender, J. F.; Hullin, E.; and Rasmussen, A. F., Jr.: The influence of avoidance-learning stress on resistance to Coxsackie B. virus in mice. *J. Immunol.* 91: 569-75, 1963.

Johnson, T., and Rasmussen, A. F., Jr.: Emotional stress and susceptibility to poliomyelitis virus infection in mice. *Arch. Ges. Virus Forsch.* 18: 392-98, 1965.

Kimmel, H. D.: Instrumental conditioning of autonomically mediated responses in human beings. *Amer. Psychol.* 29: 325-35, 1974.

Levine, S., and Cohen, C.: Differential survival to leukemia as a function of infantile stimulation in DBA/Z mice. *Proc. Soc. Exp. Biol. Med.* 102: 53-54, 1959.

Lowenstein, F. W.: Blood-pressure in relation to age and sex in the tropics and subtropics. *Lancet* 1: 389-92, 1961.

Lown, B.; Verrier, R.; and Corbalan, R.: Psychologic stress and threshold for repetitive ventricular response. *Science* 182: 834-36, 1973.

Marsh, J. T.; Lavender, J. F.; Chang, S. S.; and Rasmussen, A. F., Jr.: Poliomyelitis in monkeys: decreased susceptibility after avoidance stress. *Science* 140: 1414-15, 1963.

Miller, N. E.: Liberalization of basic S-R concepts: extensions to conflict behavior, motivation, and social learning. In *Psychology: A Study of a Science*, Study 1, Vol. 2, ed. S. Koch. New York: McGraw-Hill, 1959.

————: Learning resistance to pain and fear: effects of overlearning, exposure, and rewarded exposure in context. *J. Exp. Psychol.* 60: 137-45, 1960.

————: Animal experiments on emotionally-induced ulcers. In *Proc. World Congress of Psychiatry* (June 4-10, 1961, Montreal), Vol. 3. Toronto: University of Toronto Press, 1963.

————: Behavioral and physiological techniques: rationale and experimental designs for combining their use. In *Handbook of Physiology*, Section 6, Vol. 1, ed. C. F. Code and W. Heidel. Baltimore: Williams & Wilkins, 1967.

————: Learning of visceral and glandular responses. *Science* 163: 434-45, 1969.

————: A psychologist's perspective on neural and psychological mechanisms in cardiovascular disease. In *Neural and Psychological Mechanisms in Cardiovascular Disease*, ed. A. Zanchetti. Milan: Casa Editrice, Il Ponte, 1972a.

————: Learning of visceral and glandular responses: postscript. In *Current Status of Physiological Psychology*, ed. D. Singh and C. T. Morgan. Monterey: Brooks/Cole, 1972b.

_____: Applications of learning and biofeedback to psychiatry and medicine. In *Comprehensive Textbook of Psychiatry*, 2, ed. A. M. Freedman, H. I. Kaplan, and B. J. Sadock. Baltimore: Williams & Wilkins, 1975.

_____: Fact and fancy about biofeedback and its clinical implications. In *Catalogue of Selected Documents in Psychology*, 6. Washington: American Psychological Association, 1976.

Miller, N. E., and Carmona, A.: Modification of a visceral response, salivation in thirsty dogs, by instrumental training with water reward. *J. Comp. Physiol. Psychol.* 63: 1-6, 1967.

Miller, N. E.; DiCara, L. V.; and Wolf, G.: Homeostasis and reward: T-maze learning induced by manipulating anti-diuretic hormone. *Amer. J. Physiol.* 215: 684-86, 1968.

Miller, N. E., and Dworkin, B. R.: Visceral learning: recent difficulties with curarized rats and significant problems for human research. In *Cardiovasular Psychophysiology*, ed. P. A. Obrist, A. H. Black, J. Brener, and L. V. DiCara. Chicago: Aldine, 1974.

_____: Effects of learning on visceral functions: biofeedback. *New Engl. J. Med.* 296: 1274-78, 1977a.

_____: Critical issues in therapeutic applications of biofeedback. In *Biofeedback: Theory and Research*, ed. G. E. Schwartz and J. Beatty. New York: Academic Press, 1977b.

Myers, A. K.: The effects of predictable vs. unpredictable punishment in the albino rat. Ph.D. thesis, Yale University, 1956.

Overmeir, J. B., and Seligman, M.E.P.: Effects of inescapable shock upon subsequent escape and avoidance responding. *J. Comp. Physiol. Psychol.* 63: 28-33, 1967.

Pavlov, I. P.: *Conditioned Reflexes*. Translated by G. V. Anrep. London: Oxford University Press, 1927. Reprint. New York: Dover, 1960.

Pickering, T. G.; Brucker, B.; Frankel, H. L.; Mathias, C. J.; Dworkin, B. R.; and Miller, N. E.: Mechanisms of learned voluntary control of blood pressure in patients with generalized bodily paralysis. In *Biofeedback and Behavior: A NATO Symposium*, ed. J. Beatty and H. Legewie. New York: Plenum Press, 1977.

Pickering, T. G., and Miller, N. E.: Learned voluntary control of heart rate and rhythm in two subjects with premature ventricular contractions. *Brit. Heart J.* 39: 152-59, 1977.

Rasmussen, A. F., Jr: Emotions and immunity. *Ann. N. Y. Acad. Sci.* 164: 458-62, 1969.

Rasmussen, A. F., Jr.; Marsh, J. T.; and Brill, N. Q.: Increased susceptibility to Herpes simplex in mice subjected to avoidance-learning stress or restraint. *Proc. Soc. Exp. Biol. Med.* 96: 183-89, 1957.

Rasmussen, A. F., Jr.; Spence, E. T.; and Marsh, J. T.: Decrease in susceptibility of mice to passive anaphylaxis following avoidance-learning stress. *Proc. Soc. Exp. Biol. Med.* 100: 878-79, 1959.

Richter, C.: On the phenomenon of sudden death in animals and man. *Psychosom. Med.* 19: 191-98, 1957.

Rothfield, B.; Paré, W. P.; Varady, A.; Isom, K. E.; and Karmon, A.: The effects of environmental stress on cholesterol synthesis and metabolism. *Biochem. Med.* 7: 292-98, 1973.

Schildkraut, J. J.: *Neuropsychopharmacology and the Affective Disorders.* Boston: Little, Brown, 1969.

Seligman, M.E.P., and Maier, S. F.: Failure to escape traumatic shock. *J. Exp. Psychol.* 74: 1-9, 1967.

Shapiro, A. P., and Melhado, J.: Factors affecting development of hypertensive vascular disease after renal injury in rats. *Proc. Soc. Exp. Biol. Med.* 96: 619-23, 1957.

Shapiro, A. P.; Schwartz, G. E.; Ferguson, D.C.E.; Redmond, D. P.; and Weiss, S. M.: Behavioral methods in the treatment of hypertension. I. Review of their clinical status. *Ann. Int. Med.* 1977, in press.

Shapiro, D.; Tursky, B.; and Schwartz, G. E.: Differentiation of heart rate and systolic blood pressure in man by operant conditioning. *Psychosom. Med.* 32: 417-23, 1970.

Shapiro, M. M., and Herendeen, D. L.: Food-reinforced inhibition of conditioned salivation in dogs. *J. Comp. Physiol. Psychol.* 88: 628:32, 1975.

Swazey, J. P.: *Chlorpromazine in Psychiatry: A Study of Therapeutic Innovation.* Cambridge, Mass.: MIT Press, 1974.

Vessey, S. H.: Effects of grouping on levels of circulating antibodies in mice. *Proc. Soc. Exp. Biol. Med.* 115: 252-55, 1964.

Weiss, J. M.: Effects of coping responses on stress. *J. Comp. Physiol. Psychol.* 65: 251-60, 1968.

_____ : Somatic effects of predictable and unpredictable shock. *Psychosom. Med.* 32: 397-408, 1970.

_____ : Effects of coping behavior in different warning signal conditions on stress pathology in rats. *J. Comp. Physiol. Psychol.* 77: 1-13, 1971a.

_____ : Effects of punishing the coping response (conflict) on stress pathology in rats. *J. Comp. Physiol. Psychol.* 77: 14-21, 1971b.

_____ : Psychological factors in stress and disease. *Sci. Amer.* 226, 6:104-13, 1972.

Weiss, J. M.; and Glazer, H. I.: Effects of acute exposure to stressors on subsequent avoidance-escape behavior. *Psychosom. Med.* 37: 499-521, 1975.

Weiss, J. M.; Glazer, H. I.; and Pohorecky, L. A.: Coping behavior and neurochemical changes: an alternative explanation for the original "learned helplessness" hypothesis. In *Animal Models in Human Psychobiology*, ed. G. Serban and A. Kling. New York: Plenum Press, 1976.

Weiss, J. M.; Glazer, H. I.; Pohorecky, L. A.; Brick, J.; and Miller, N. E.: Effects of chronic exposure to stressors on avoidance-escape behavior and on brain norepinephrine. *Psychosom. Med.* 37: 522-34, 1975.

Weiss, J. M.; Stone, E. A.; and Harrell, N.: Coping behavior and brain norepinephrine level in rats. *J. Comp. Physiol. Psychol.* 72: 153-60, 1970.

Wistar, R. T., and Hildemann, W. H.: Effect of stress on skin transplantation immunity in mice. *Science* 131: 159-60, 1960.

Yamada, A.; Jensen, M.; and Rasmussen, A. F., Jr.: Stress and susceptibility to viral infections. III. Antibody response and viral retention during avoidance learning stress. *Proc. Soc. Exp. Biol. Med.* 116: 677-80, 1964.

V

SOMATOPSYCHIC EFFECTS
OF INTEROCEPTION

John I. Lacey and Beatrice C. Lacey *

The autonomic nervous system is treated, in the body of our textbooks, almost entirely as an effector system. Mitchell (1953), a distinguished student of the anatomy of the autonomic nervous sytem, rightfully characterizes such treatments as "irrational." For in the body of an animal, the picture is rather different than that given in most textbooks. Consider that, in the cat, more than 24,000 of the 30,000 fibers in the cervical vagus are sensory afferents (Agostoni et al. 1957). Similarly, 50 percent of the 28,000 splanchnic fibers are afferent, and afferent fibers constitute 90 percent of the rabbit's abdominal vagus.

Such numerical prominence surely implies functional significance. Moreover, it is increasingly clear that the significance of visceral afferent systems is not defined and delimited by their role as transmitters of primary sensory information from the viscera to the central nervous system. Stimulation of visceral afferents produces *nonsensory* effects on brain activity, just as does stimulation of the more familiar somatic afferents.

Chase and Sterman and their colleagues (Chase et al. 1967; Chase, Sterman, and Clemente 1966) have provided some pointed examples. They found that stimulation of afferent fibers in the abdominal vagus desynchronized the electrical activity of cortex and thalamus and evoked theta activity in the hippocampus. Such effects commonly are associated with alertness, wakefulness, "arousal," or "activation." Stimulation of the cervical vagus,

*Fels Professors of Psychiatry/The Fels Research Institute/Wright State University/ Yellow Springs, Ohio

however, yielded *either* synchronizing *or* desynchronizing effects, depending on stimulus parameters. Study of the evoked potential complex along the vagus nerve demonstrated that these different effects were mediated by separable fiber systems, characterizable by different thresholds and different fiber size (and, hence, different conduction speeds). Different visceral afferents, it may be concluded, may have opposing effects on the brain.

Gahery and Vigier (1974) have recently published a dramatic example of the far-reaching and unexpected effects produced by stimulation of visceral afferents. Stimulation of the vago-aortic afferent fibers was able to obliterate completely any evoked potentials in the nucleus cuneatus, a primary relay station along the somesthetic pathway. The effect was demonstrated to depend on presynaptic inhibition. Stimulation of vago-aortic afferents, then, presynaptically prevented the normal response to sensory input! Such stimulation resulted, in a phrase we have used often, in an effective "rejection" of external environmental inputs. Gahery and Vigier conclude cautiously that their data "suggest that vago-aortic afferents are not limited to a vegetative role, but may also be involved in a variety of physiological regulations."

The cardiovascular afferents constitute an important part of the vago-aortic afferent pathways. For the past fourteen years we have concentrated on demonstrations of the possible role of these afferents in behavior. We have tried to uncover new phenomena in intact man that would be congruent with the many neurophysiological discoveries that increasingly demand a reevaluation of traditional notions concerning the role of blood pressure and heart rate in behavior.

Put very briefly, our guiding hypothesis is that *decreases* in blood pressure and heart rate facilitate sensory reception and sensorimotor integration, whereas *increases* in blood pressure and heart rate blunt (and may even obliterate) sensory reception; they can degrade sensorimotor intergration, and they favor internalized cognitive activities involving storage into, retrieval from, and manipulation of the contents of memory. We hypothesize that these effects are attributable to the nonsensory effects on the brain of impulse traffic along the cardiovascular afferents.

We early demonstrated (Lacey et al. 1963; Lacey and Lacey 1970) that situations requiring simply attending to external environmental events were accompanied by preparatory or concomitant bradycardia and hypotension, whereas situations either involving painful stimulation or requiring inattention to or active rejection of external stimulation in favor of "mental concentration" produced the opposite effects: elevations in blood pressure and heart rate. Other simultaneously recorded variables, such as respiration and electrodermal activity, did *not* differentiate the two sets of task requirements. We found also (Lacey and Lacey 1970) that the preparatory interval in a reaction time situation (the interval between a warning stimulus and the actual delivery of the stimulus to respond) was characterized by anticipatory beat-by-beat cardiac decelerations that ended only when the imperative stimulus was delivered. The deceleration was not attributable to either blood pressure or respiratory changes. Moreover, reaction time was *faster* the *greater the deceleration and the lower the final heart rate*. The correlations were not high, being of the order of -0.2 to -0.4 in different experiments and subjects. It is their direction, not their magnitude, that was surprising and, of course, theoretically significant, for the direction was totally unpredictable by arousal theory.

There are now many other such correlational studies demonstrating the implied relationship (e.g., Connor and Lang 1969; Duncan-Johnson and Coles 1974; Holloway and Parsons 1972; Obrist, Webb, and Sutterer 1969). Moreover, other investigators have applied the hypothesis to such clinically important areas as gerontology, perinatal and infantile development, shizophrenia, sociopathy, hypertension, mental retardation, and even biofeedback, with, to our sympathetic eyes, encouraging results.

But there is continuing controversy over whether such correlations are to be interpreted in terms of visceral afferent theory or by some more indirect, and, in our opinion, far less satisfactory manner. Proof is still lacking. The neurophysiological effects have been described in drugged, anesthetized, surgically compromised animals. Extrapolation to the intact human is hazardous and difficult. We have failed so far to develop analogues in the intact cat of the behavior and relationships we have observed in man. But we are now encouraged by the new findings we will report here, and we will shortly return to the intact behaving cat or monkey in which, by suitable pharmacological and neurological intervention, we can hope to prove the role of cardiovascular afferents. With these acknowledgments, let us turn to a brief review of the basic neurophysiology on which we base our speculations and from which we draw our experimental designs.

The cardiovascular afferents originate in strategically scattered specialized areas along the arterial tree where there are found concentrations of receptors (the so-called baroreceptors) that respond with exquisite sensitivity to the distention and relaxation of the arterial wall that occur, to greater or lesser degree, with each systole and diastole of the cardiac cycle and that convey back to the central nervous system continuous information about the blood pressure and heart rate. The information conveyed has both an episodic, or a.c., component, due to the episodically recurring pulse wave, and a d.c. component, due to the overall averaged levels of blood pressure and heart rate.

There are several sets of such fiber systems, but the two major systems originate in the carotid sinus and in the aortic arch. The afferent fibers project to bulbar levels by the glosso-pharyngeal and vagus nerves. These pathways, as is well known, underlie a powerful and elegant reflex mechanism for the homeostatic regulation of cardiovascular activity; the cardiovascular afferents serve as a negative feedback loop, the effect of which is to restrain and dampen cardiovascular changes.

But increased activity of the cardiovascular afferents has long been known to have effects on other than cardiovascular processes. The already cited results by Gahery and Vigier, by Chase et al., and by Chase, Sterman, and Clemente are only the latest in a fairly long list. Included in the list are such suggestive facts as that, for example, increases in intra-sinusal pressure or stimulation of the carotid sinus and aortic nerves results in (1) decreased muscle tone; (2) elevation of the threshold for a mono-synaptic reflex; (3) synchronization or "disactivation" of the electrocorticogram; (4) shortened duration of motor and cortical and noncardiovascular autonomic responses; (5) instant termination of episodes of sham rage in the acutely decorticated cat. It is from such neurophysiological demonstrations that we extrapolated our psychophysiological hypotheses.

An important cautionary note is needed. It can not be expected that blood pressure and heart rate changes will always and inevitably have the consequences just sketched and implied. For one thing, the baroreceptors are misnamed: they do not respond truly to changes in pressure. The truly effective stimulus to these receptors is stretch or strain. It is the deformation of the arterial wall by the ascending pressure wave that causes firing of the baroreceptor nerves. Any condition that renders the arterial wall less elastic and less capable of deformation will make the ascending pressure wave less effective as a stimulus. The elasticity of the arterial wall itself is determined by a multiplicity of factors, some accompanying normal processes of aging, some determined by pathological conditions, and some acutely determined in a normal physiological manner by sympathetic contributions to the carotid sinus, for example, which produce a stiffening of the sinusal wall. Moreover, even if arterial elasticity is held constant, the shape and effectiveness of the pulse wave when it finally arrives at the baroreceptors is modified by a variety of interrelated factors: the rate of rise and fall of the intrasinusal pressure wave, the stroke volume, the rate of injection by the left ventricle of blood into the arterial system, the rate at which blood is moved from the arteries into the capillaries, the length of the pathway from the left ventricle to the baroreceptors, peripheral resistance, and the elastic recoil of the arteries.

A final complication, of great significance to the study of the physiology of behavior, is introduced by the fact that the baroreceptor reflexes are modulated by suprabulbar mechanisms. They can be augmented or inhibited by stimulation of the central gray, mescencephalic reticular formation, posterior hypothalamus, amygdala, hippocampus, and other structures. We do not know enough about the dynamics of such effects to be able to define the physiological role of such suprabulbar mediation. But if we believe that behavior is indeed explicable by brain mechanisms, we must also believe that variations in task-requirements will be accompanied by variations in the dynamic interplay and participation of central neural structures; and that, therefore, there must be describable and reproducible circumstances in which the role of blood pressure and heart rate in determining brain activity (and, hence, behavior) will be augmented and still other circumstances in which their role will be attenuated and obliterated. The trick is to devise—or, to be more honest, to stumble upon—suitable experimental designs that will throw the anticipated phenomena into prominence. We may have stumbled upon just such a set of experimental circumstances, and it is these we report on here.

Until recently we have concentrated on the processes of cardiac deceleration and acceleration. When do they appear? What are their correlations with behavior? Such studies are subject to considerable interpretive uncertainty and controversy. We have now shifted from a preoccupation with heart rate changes to the study of time-varying effects on behavior within the *single* cardiac cycle. The results are rather dramatic and unexpected, and they provide far less maneuvering room for alternative theoretical interpretations.

Time-Varying Effects on Behavior
Within the Single Cardiac Cycle

Each cardiac cycle produces a wave of increasing and decreasing intra-arterial pressure. Taken in its least relaxed, most absolute, and strictest form, our theory seems to demand that there should be circumstances in which we should find relative behavioral inhibition early in the cardiac cycle, during the rising phase of pressure, and relative facilitation late in the cycle, during the falling phase of pressure. There have been several reports of just such phenomena, and many investigators take their occurrence—or non-occurrence—as decisive tests of the theory. There is now, however, a most respectable and sizable literature, dealing mainly with reaction time and signal detection experiments, in which there has been a complete failure to find such effects. We reject the notion that the demonstration of these phenomena is essential to our theory, for such cardiovascular-behavioral correlations deal only with the a.c. component of cardiovascular feedback and not with the d.c. component.

Obviously, however, positive evidence of such cardiac cycle effects would be of the utmost theoretical significance. We ourselves have repeatedly failed to find such positive evidence, until recently.

The clues to effective experimental designs are scattered and few, but two of them are worth reviewing here.

Tripp (1967), in an unpublished doctoral dissertation, undertook to confirm some of our early observations concerning the differential occurrence of cardiac deceleration or acceleration, depending on task requirements. The confirmation was successful. But more significantly, it turns out, he added eye-blink measurements to his recording battery.

Eye-blinks are an important "reflexive" cleansing mechanism. But the major contributions to the frequency of eye-blinks have been shown to be central in origin. The facial nucleus (VIIth nerve) has ubiquitous connections with many other parts of the central nervous system, including oculomotor nuclei, sensory trigimenal nuclei, the superior colliculi, basal ganglia, hypothalamus, and the precentral gyrus of the cortex—and with the nucleus of the tractus solitarius, the first relay station for the cardiovascular afferents.

Tripp recorded the blink rate during the performance of different tasks. He found, pooling the data over all tasks, that indeed there was a non-uniform distribution of eye-blinks over the cardiac cycle. In Figure 5.1 we have redrawn and reanalyzed Tripp's data. The two curves are for eight female subjects (solid line) and eight male subjects (broken line) and show the distribution of the absolute number of recorded eye-blinks by relative positions (by

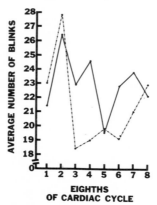

Figure 5.1. Data for eight male subjects (broken line) and eight female subjects (solid line) show that eye-blinks occur with different frequencies at different times within the cardiac cycle.

Source: R. M. Tripp, A study of cardiac afferent influence on an involuntary motor behavior: a determinant of blinking (Ph.D. thesis, Duke University), 1967.

eighths) within the cardiac cycle. For both sexes there can be seen to be nonlinear trends. Blinks are relatively infrequent in the very early part of the cardiac cycle, increase sharply in the second eighth of the cycle, and then diminish again. Analyzed by Ferguson's nonparametric trend test (Ferguson 1965) a significant two-branched segmentally monotonic function is found for both sexes pooled and for the male subjects alone. Tripp's study has hidden within it two important clues: (1) it deals with what we shall call *episodically emitted* behavior, appearing irregularly at internally generated intervals; and (2) the effects are nonlinear within the cardiac cycle.

These clues again emerge in a small pilot study by Forsyth (1966). Figure 5.2 is drawn from Forsyth's tabulated data, and again we reanalyzed the data by Ferguson's nonparametric trend test. The graph shows, for each of three tests approximately one month apart, the distribution of lever presses within the cardiac cycle, for one monkey, on a Sidman avoidance schedule. On the first and second tests, shown by the two bottom lines, irregularly shaped curves can be seen, with more lever presses early and late in the cardiac cycle. The third tests, shown in the topmost panel, is based on a longer recording session. This more extensive set of data shows a three-branched segmentally monotonic characteristic—Ferguson's tritonic curve. The tritonicity is significant at below the 0.02 level. Lever presses increase, decrease, and

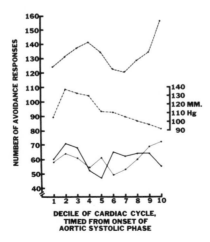

Figure 5.2. Data for one monkey on a Sidman avoidance schedule show that avoidance responses occur with different frequencies at different times within the cardiac cycle. From top to bottom: results for a long recording session, three months after testing began; average blood pressure curve; results for two shorter recording sessions, approximately one month apart.

then finally increase sharply in the later part of the cycle, when blood pressure is at its lowest level.

The average blood pressure curve simultaneously secured is shown in the center panel. It appears that sometime after the occurrence of the blood pressure peak (that is, after a transmission delay) there is a depression of the rate of responding, which is followed by a sharp recovery. In terms of our model, the inhibitory impulses originating in the carotid sinus and aortic arch control the time of occurrence of episodically emitted behavior, behavior that again appears after internally generated intervals.

The question now arises: What sorts of emitted behaviors should we study in pursuit of our specific hypotheses? All our previous work suggests, first, that the task to be used should involve internal preparation for an integrated sensorimotor act. Second, the task should be one in which the internal preparation would be accompanied by cardiac deceleration progressively increasing in time. The reason for this specification rests on intuition and remote inference from some negative results. Given the appropriate experimental context, the appearance of cardiac deceleration is to us a suggestion that the central nervous system is operating in such a way that baroreceptor discharge will be *allowed* to become effective as part of a negative feedback loop to the brain.

We determined, accordingly, that we would study *episodically emitted motor responses, which functioned to gate in sensory inputs.*

We followed this prescription in two separate experiments. In each, the subjects emitted responses after self-generated preparatory intervals. In each experiment the emitted responses caused the appearance of visual stimuli of some significance to the subject. We expected—or rather hoped—to find, first, that cardiac deceleration would precede the motor response, and, second, that the emitted motor response would not occur randomly in time throughout the cardiac cycle. In both experiments we found the anticipated preparatory cardiac deceleration. In neither experiment did we find the predicted nonrandom occurrence of motor events within the cardiac cycle.

And, then, slowly, the lights blinked on! We were ignoring our own warnings that individual pressure waves varied in their effectiveness as stimuli to the baroreceptors. Reference to the details of the temporal distribution of baroreceptor discharges led to predictions that we were able to support with clarity in both experiments.

The temporal distribution of baroreceptor discharge is not invariant. Many experiments have shown that baroreceptor discharge normally occurs in sporadic bursts, temporally correlated with the rise and fall of intrasinusal pressure. But the temporal distribution of baroreceptor discharge through the cardiac cycle can be observed to vary widely. The nerve can fire abruptly with a peaked and narrow temporal distribution, or the distribution can be broad and flat, with considerable temporal dispersion. At high levels of heart rate and blood pressure the nerve can be observed to fire continuously through the entire cardiac cycle, in which case, of course, there could not be any cardiac cycle effect. Powerful abstract tools of engineering analysis have been applied by many investigators to such phenomena. If the time course of a *single* pressure cycle is considered to be the forcing function, the differential equation that closely predicts temporal firing pattern includes separate terms for rate of pressure increase, rate of pressure fall, and mean pressure thresholds. When frequency of intracarotid pulsatile change is added and a frequency domain analysis is performed, two frequency-dependent measures emerge: *gain* and *phase shift*. As frequency increases, the gain of the baroreceptor feedback loop increases; that is, the amplitude of the time-varying wave of firing frequency increases. As frequency increases, phase-shift also increases; that is, the major concentration of baroreceptor discharge is shifted forward in time. Now, frequency is the analogue of heart rate. The effect of—or the reason for—cardiac deceleration during the preparatory interval becomes clearer: when frequency decreases, the gain and phase shift of the baroreceptor feedback loop decrease; baroreceptor discharge shows a narrower temporal distribution, and there is more "safe time" during the cardiac cycle, during which there will be less interference with sensorimotor performance. As heart rate increases, a larger and larger portion of the earlier part of each cardiac cycle would be occupied by higher frequency firing of cardiovascular afferents, and the favored time for the emission of responses would be displaced to later and later parts of the cardiac cycle. At very high rates there should be no safe time left at all, and responses should be emitted randomly within the cardiac cycle. In what we hope is a suggestive phrase: a.c. (or cardiac cycle) effects should depend on the concomitant d.c. (or momentary heart rate) level.

These predictions were well satisfied by the experimental data.

In the first study fifty-two subjects worked on what is known as a drl 15"lh4" schedule. That is, they had to press a key no earlier than fifteen seconds and no later than nineteen seconds after their previous press in order to be successful. Whether the press was successful or unsuccessful was signaled to the subject by the appearance of a brief automatically activated visual display. We continued the experiment until each subject had executed sixty successful trials.

For each of the sixty trials we determined the heart rate of the cardiac cycle that just *preceded* the cycle in which the response occurred, thus estimating heart rate level uncontaminated by the actual execution of the sensorimotor act. The trials were then divided into five equal categories on the basis of pre-press heart rate level, and the median value of relative time-of-press within the cardiac cycle was determined for each category of the heart rate distributions. Figure 5.3 shows the results for the subjects, broken down into three groups: slow heart rate subjects, middle heart rate subjects, and fast heart rate subjects.

On the Y-axis are plotted the group averages of individual median relative response times. On the X-axis are plotted the quintiles of heart rate level; the first quintile comprises the lowest 20 percent of the heart rates, and the fifth quintile comprises the highest 20 percent of the heart rates. There is a wide-ranging trend for the slow heart rate subjects, significant at below the 0.05 level. As heart rate increases, the favored time of response is indeed shifted to later and later parts of the cardiac cycle. For middle heart rate subjects there is a somewhat more constricted range, but a significant trend (at the 0.01 level) is again seen: as heart rate increases, the favored time of response is shifted to later and later parts of the cardiac cycle. For the fast heart rate subjects in whom it would be expected that the baroreceptor discharge would be more nearly continuous through the entire cardiac cycle, there is a very restricted range of variation, and there is no significant trend.

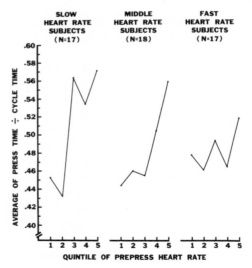

Figure 5.3. The relationship of heart rate level to relative time of press for fifty-two subjects. The subjects were divided into three subgroups on the basis of their median prepress heart rate. For both slow and middle heart rate subjects, time of response occurs later in the cycle as heart rate increases. Fast heart rate subjects show no such dependency.

A second experiment was then performed in order to generalize these results. In this experiment the subjects, at their own pace and volition, raised their finger from a resting spot. This episodically emitted behavior after internally generally preparatory intervals resulted immediately and automatically in a very brief exposure of a schematic clock face outlined by light emitting diodes. The subjects' task was to report which light was not illuminated. Twenty subjects participated, with 175 trials each.

In analyzing the cardiac cycle effect in this experiment we introduced an additional kind of analysis specifically directed to the problem of nonlinear effects, which appeared to a striking degree in this experiment. The previous experiment was analyzed only in terms of the central tendency of the response times—namely, the group average of individual median response times. What is needed is intensive study of individual distributions of response times, with particular attention to the details of the shape of the frequency distributions. To study this in any detail, we would need a very large number of responses at each of many heart rate levels in a sizable number of individuals. We have not yet performed such a heroic experiment. But, as a beginning of such an enterprise, we have analyzed the frequency-dependency of three measures of location—the 25th, 50th, and 75th percentile points of the distribution of relative response times. Our question is whether each of these values equally well reflects the interaction of heart rate with time of response. In other words, is the displacement toward larger delays as heart rate increases uniform for the whole distribution, or is there any evidence for skewed effects?

Again the preresponse heart rate levels, uncontaminated by the response itself, were used to form fifths of heart rate distribution; the quartile response times for each subject were determined for each heart rate category; and, finally, the results were averaged over subjects. The subjects were divided into two groups: the ten subjects with the fastest heart rates and the ten subjects with the slowest heart rates. Figure 5.4 shows the results.

To interpret this figure, look first at the center panels in the top and bottom halves of the figure, labeled Q2. In these panels are plotted the results for the median response times for the slow and fast heart rate subjects, in the same manner as in the previous experiment. The slow heart rate subjects show a marked nonlinearity. While the latest response times do occur at the highest rates, there is a dip in the curve in the second quintile of heart rate. This bitonic trend is significant at the 0.05 level. The dip is inexplicable as yet in terms of the details of our model. We assume heuristically that it is due to unknown nonlinearities of the characteristics of baroreceptor discharge at very low heart rates. Such nonlinearities are known, in general, to exist in baroreceptor discharge, and studies of the frequency dependency of baroreceptor discharge commonly limit their quantitative formulations to the range of linear effects.

By contrast, the fast heart rate subjects again show a restricted range of effect of heart rate on response time, as in the previous experiment, and no trend test (monotonic, bitonic, or tritonic) yielded statistical significance.

The left-most panels, both top and bottom, labeled Q1, show the results when the 25th percentile of the frequency distribution is used as the dependent variable, and the right-most panels, labelled Q3, show the results for the 75th percentile. The question being asked is whether the frequency dependency of response time is manifest throughout the distribution of response time. If it is, then Q1, Q2, and Q3 should all behave alike, both qualitatively and quantitatively. For slow heart rate subjects the curves are alike, both in shape and in the magnitude of effect, for all three measures, although they achieve significance only for the median or Q2 value. We may

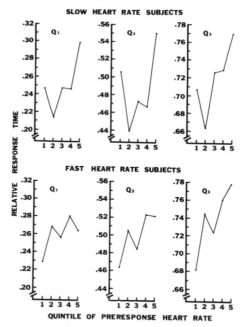

Figure 5.4. Relative response time as a function of preresponse heart rate level, plotted separately for each quartile of the dependent variable. Data are for twenty subjects divided into slow and fast heart rate groups. For slow heart rate subjects, frequency dependency of response time is approximately the same whether Q1, Q2, or Q3 of response times is plotted. For fast heart rate subjects, the range of effect increases from Q1 to Q2 to Q3.

conclude that the frequency dependencies of all three measures are essentially alike.

For fast heart rate subjects a somewhat different conclusion seems justified. Although the shapes of the Q1, Q2, and Q3 curves are similar, they vary widely in the range of effect shown, with an increasing effect from Q1 to Q3. The Q1 and Q2 curves do not yield significance; but the monotonic trend for Q3 is significant at the 0.02 level. The suggestion is fascinating: for fast heart rate subjects, only responses occurring very late in the cardiac cycle (where there still may be some "safe time") show significant nonrandomness; only these later responses show a systematic relationship to heart rate. In other words, for fast heart rate subjects most of the cardiac cycle is accompanied by inhibitory baroreceptor discharge, and response times are not determined very strongly by momentary variations of heart rate around the already high heart rate level. Whether the very late portion of the cardiac cycle also is accompanied by inhibitory discharge, however, still depends markedly on the momentary heart rate variations, and in this late portion of the curve we can again detect, with satisfactory statistical significance, the hypothesized nonrandomness of emitted behavior and its frequency dependency.

These data confirm the most general form of the hypothesis that the time at which behaviors are emitted within the cardiac cycle is not random but is determined by the momentary level of heart rate. As heart rate increases, responses are delayed to later and later phases of the cardiac cycle. The trend is more marked at lower than at higher heart rates. The data also support the concept that the effect is nonlinear: there is not simply an upward shift of response times, symmetrical throughout the time distribution. Rather, there seem to be differential changes in the different moments of the frequency distribution of response times. These changes are congruent with what is known about the temporal distribution of baroreceptor discharge. The bitonic trends seen for slow heart rate subjects and the differences between slow and fast heart rate subjects suggest nonlinearities, in the range of very low heart rates, in the temporal distribution of baroreceptor discharge in addition to those already described in the studies dealing with acute animal preparations.

We are almost tempted to say, Q.E.D. But there are still some difficulties. First is the fact that we started this paper with an appeal to the proposition that the numerosity of visceral afferents argues for their functional importance. But our interpretation of the findings of our experiments can be attacked on this very basis because, despite the most vigorous search by many highly competent neurophysiologists, only a few neurons can be found in and around the nucleus of the tractus solitarius that discharge synchronously with the pulse, although many neurons respond to changes in blood pressure more prolonged than those produced by each cardiac cycle. There can be many reasons: either the search has been in the wrong place; or, because so many influences converge on the target neurons, only averaging techniques will suffice to reveal pulse-synchronous discharge. But the evidence now suggests to us that controls need to be instituted in these neurophysiological experiments for frequency dependency. The experiments are commonly performed under anesthetics and other drugs that produce high heart rate levels, under which circumstances we would not expect to find pulse synchrony of neuronal discharge.

A second difficulty arises because our predictions concerning the effect of heart rate level derive from studies in which sine waves of different frequencies were used as forcing functions to the carotid sinus. But when sine waves are used, there is a perfect correlation between frequency and rates of rise and fall of intracarotid pressure, and the rate of change is known to be one of the most important determinants of baroreceptor discharge. We are now trying to demonstrate frequency dependency of baroreceptor discharge using waves with fixed rates of rise and fall at all frequencies.

Until these questions are resolved satisfactorily, we can not maintain anything other than that we have demonstrated variations of emitted behavior within the cardiac cycle that may, however, depend on mechanisms other than those we favor. But we, at least, cannot think of any other mechanisms. It is our belief that these findings narrow the field of possible theoretical explanations and that visceral afferent theory remains the most likely explanation.

Given our rate of progress over the past fourteen years, there is much work to be done in the future. In the meantime, we reassert the main elements of our hypothesis: baroreceptor discharge is inhibitory to sensorimotor activity and is facilitatory of internalized cognitive activities. In this notion we find a basis for understanding the physiological reason for, or at least the physiological consequences of, the fact that the heart decelerates and the blood pressure goes down when detection of, and response to, external stimuli is required; whereas, when such stimuli are the objects of what we may call "motivated inattention," heart rate and blood pressure go up. Among other effects, as the data suggest, the deceleration allows freer and temporally more extended deployment by the subject, within the cardiac cycle, of his perceiving and responding activities.

References

Agostoni, E.; Chinnock, J. E.; Daly, M. D.; and Murray, J. G.: Functional and histological studies on the vagus and its branches of the heart, lungs, and abdominal viscera in the cat. *J. Physiol.* (London) 135: 182-205, 1957.

Chase, M. H.; Nakamura, Y.; Cemente, C. D.; and Sterman, M. B.: Afferent vagal stimulation: neurographic correlates of induced EEG synchronization and desynchronization. *Brain Res.* 5: 236-49, 1967.

Chase, M. H.; Sterman, M. B.; and Clemente, C. D.: Cortical and subcortical patterns of response to afferent vagal stimulation. *Exper. Neurol.* 16: 36-49, 1966.

Connor, W. H., and Lang, P. J.: Cortical slow-wave and cardiac rate response in stimulus orientation and reaction time conditions. *J. Exper. Psychol.* 82: 310-20, 1969.

Duncan-Johnson, C. C., and Coles, M.G.H.: Heart rate and disjunctive reaction time: the effects of discrimination requirements. *J. Exper. Psychol.* 103: 1160-68, 1974.

Ferguson, G. A.: *Nonparametric Trend Analyses.* Montreal: McGill University Press, 1965.

Forsyth, R. M.: Influence of blood pressure on patterns of voluntary behavior. *Psychophysiol.* 2: 98-102, 1966.

Gahery, Y., and Vigier, D.: Inhibitory effects in the cuneate nucleus produced by vago-aortic afferent fibers. *Brain Res.* 75: 241-46, 1974.

Holloway, F. A., and Parsons, O. A.: Physiological concomitants of reaction time performance in normal and brain-damaged subjects. *Psychophysiol.* 9: 189-98, 1972.

Lacey, J. I.; Kagan, J.; Lacey, B. C.; and Moss, H. A.: The visceral level: situational determinants and behavioral correlates of autonomic response patterns. In *Expression of the Emotions in Man,* ed. P. H. Knapp. New York: International Universities Press, 1963.

Lacey, J. I., and Lacey, B. C.: Some autonomic-central nervous system interrelationships. In *Physiological Correlates of Emotion,* ed. P. Black. New York: Academic Press, 1970.

Mitchell, G.A.G.: *Anatomy of the Autonomic Nervous System.* London: E. and S. Livingstone, 1953.

Obrist, P. A.; Webb, R. A.; and Sutterer, J. R.: Heart rate and somatic changes during aversive conditioning and a simple reaction time task. *Psychophysiol.* 5: 696-723, 1969.

Tripp, R. M.: A study of cardiac afferent influence on an involuntary motor behavior: a determinant of blinking. Ph. D. thesis, Duke University, 1967.

VI

A CLASSIFICATION OF
AFFECTIVE DISORDERS BASED ON
A SYNTHESIS OF NEW
AND OLD CONCEPTS

Martin Roth*

Introduction

It would seem appropriate in this volume on research in psychobiology to consider the relationship between the contributions of Adolf Meyer and the work of those of his contemporaries who laid the foundations of the system of classification of mental disorder in use in most parts of the world at the present time.

Kraepelin and his followers tried to depict syndromes with a specific clinical picture, of course, and outcome, and they hoped by these means to discover the underlying pathological causes of mental disorders. The scientific value of this endeavor extended beyond such specific objectives. But his particular medical model was narrow and restrictive, paying scant attention to social, familial, and historical factors. For Adolf Meyer it appeared as an inadequate, professionally parochial foundation for the care of mentally sick people. He therefore addressed himself to the task of enlarging the vision of practicing psychiatrists by bringing to their attention a wider range of those influences that could have contributed to the individual's mental distress. Adolf Meyer succeeded in adding certain essential dimensions to clinical prac-

*Professor and Chairman of Department of Psychiatry/New Addenbrooke's Hospital/ University of Cambridge/Cambridge, England

tice that had previously been lacking. And his contributions to the practice of psychiatry and medicine have therefore been of lasting importance.

But in his disregard of classification he carried his doctrine to extremes that probably impeded the scientific approach to psychiatry. Emphasizing the individual's uniqueness, he was uninterested in "disease" entities and failed to appreciate the forward leap in knowledge represented by Kraepelin's concept of manic-depressive illness. Yet but for this advance, knowledge of affective disorder would have been not far removed from the accounts of "melancholia" handed down in the writings of such physicians as Hippocrates, and Aretaeus, such biographers as Plutarch, and that compendium of infinite variety made up of myth, fabulous conjecture, and scholarship, Burton's *Anatomy of Melancholy*.

The clinical syndromes depicted by Kraepelin have, like most good descriptions in biology and medicine, withstood the test of time. For such accounts always do more than passively reflect the features that present to the observer. They contain a conjecture about how things are in the world, stated in terms sufficiently simple, clear, and parsimonious to be tested and so refuted or upheld. Implicit in the successful description, one or more good hypotheses are to be found. As Darwin pointed out: "How odd it is that anyone should not see that all observations must be for or against some view." In this is to be found the reason for the important part played by classification and faithful description in generating new problems and promoting knowledge and understanding in all disciplines.

When biochemists, physiologists, and other basic scientists were attracted in growing numbers to the problems of mental disorder, following upon the introduction of the first pharmacotherapeutic advances of twenty-five years ago, the hope was widely entertained that a taxonomy derived from objective biochemical indices would soon supersede that derived from crude clinical investigation. Such hopes have remained unfulfilled. The discovery of the therapeutic value of lithium carbonate (Cade 1949) and the revival and reexploration of the unipolar-bipolar concept have served as reminders that good clinical observation, for all its apparent crudeness, often proves fruitful and that sound classification may be an essential precondition even for the advance of biochemical and physiological knowledge of mental disorder.

These recent developments have brought about a recrudescence of interest in diagnosis. But the wide-ranging biological and therapeutic implications of the unipolar-principle have encouraged some workers to apply it to the exclusion of all others in the classification of affective disorders. This practice is inconsistent with the original views and intentions of Leonhard (1957), who first differentiated the "monopolar" from the "bipolar" disorders and confined these concepts to the endogenous states. This clearly presupposed a prior separation of the latter forms of affective disorder. Much confusion and some discordant findings flow from the varying ways in which the unipolar-bipolar principle has been construed and applied. An attempt is therefore being made to bring observations based on such concepts as "endogenous" and "neurotic" depression and their associations with anxiety states and schizophreniform disorders into relationship with the concepts on which more attention has been focused in recent years. On the basis of this synthesis of observations from different areas, a classification of affective disorders and conditions closely related to them is tentatively suggested. It draws as far as possible upon empirical psychopathological inquiries.

The present paper is mainly devoted to the relationships between endogenous and neurotic, unipolar and bipolar depressions. The associations with anxiety and phobic states, other neurotic disorders, and schizophreniform states are also briefly examined. In the final section the relationships between different conceptual and experimental models of depression are discussed, and the possible affinities between certain models and some of the disorders depicted in this classification are considered.

A companion paper to the present one (Roth 1976a) examines the association between normal fluctuations of affect with affective disorder and looks in greater detail at the place of the unipolar and bipolar disorders and of anxiety neuroses in the scheme of the classification proposed. The association between the groupings proposed and treatment response within the affective disorders is also considered.

"Endogenous" and "Neurotic" Depressions

Although discovery and redefinition of the unipolar-bipolar concept stimulated interest in diagnosis among many who formerly regarded this as a scientifically sterile exercise, the practice adopted by some workers of substituting it for, rather than trying to integrate it with, the "psychotic-neurotic" or the "endogenous-reactive" principle has caused a certain confusion. For in some centers the unipolar concept has been given a narrow and in others a wide connotation. The situation now needs reappraisal in the light of the experience of the past decade to determine whether the advantages of the unipolar-bipolar principle in the classification of depression can be retained without jettisoning what was useful in the older concepts.

It is significant that bipolar and unipolar disorders have been widely assumed to be categorically distinct entities without formal evidence that this is the case. Yet a grey area of undefined extent exists between them. The occurrence of three separate depressive episodes demanded by Perris (1974a) for the diagnosis of "unipolar" disorders is not a very sharp criterion and leaves the status of a substantial minority of cases undecided. With morbid risks of 15 percent or less among secondary cases, heredity cannot be reckoned a precise criterion in diagnosis.

Further ambiguities arise from the fact that mild attacks of elation, whether they occur immediately after attacks of depression or between them, engender a sense of well-being and achievement; they are not complained of and are difficult to identify retrospectively. The attacks of depression that are, by far, the commonest forms of disturbed affect are not differentiated by any clear phenomenological criteria in the two groups. Such features as have been described are impressionistic and of uncertain weight. Yet the categorically distinct nature of "bipolar" or "manic-depressive" illness, in a strict sense, has been implicitly accepted by most workers, including those who defend the modern version of the continuum theory of depressive illness (Kendell 1968), although it was rejected in the unitary theory of Lewis (1934).

The reasons are likely to be that, notwithstanding some measure of ambiguity, the theory that postulates a categorical demarcation between bipolar and unipolar depressive psychoses raises refutable hypotheses for a whole range of biological approaches and is more practicable for clinical and scientific purposes. In short, it is of greater heuristic value. The history of the Leonhard concept has, therefore, a certain bearing upon the wider controversies as to whether a dimensional or a categorical approach should be adopted in the classification and diagnosis of affective disorders and psychiatric illness generally.

Both Angst and Perris (1972) have explicitly followed Leonhard in restricting the bipolar-unipolar concept to the realm of the endogenous or "vital" depressions (van Praag 1972). The alternative view, which applies the concept more generally within the area of affective disorders, is ill defined and has never been supported by evidence from systematic investigations.

If it is accepted that a categorical distinction between bipolar and unipolar depressions provides the most clear and serviceable model for classification of the "endogenous" depressions, the next question that requires resolution is whether any clear dividing line exists between the unipolar endogenous depressions and the remaining group of depressive disorders. The combined groups constitute the majority of depressed patients seen in clinical practice. And they continue to be denoted in many European, some North American centers, and most official systems of classification (ICD-8, 1968) by means of such terms as *neurotic* or *reactive*. The alternative to this categorical view is that one regards the endogenous and neurotic forms of illness as different points along a single continuum, namely a "psychotic-neurotic" dimension (Kendell 1968). The implications for classification of such continuum or dimensional concepts of the endogenous and neurotic depressions extend beyond the depressive states, for any arguments in favor of dimensional concepts for the depressive disorders would apply a fortiori to the neuroses, where the work of the Slaters (Slater and Slater 1944) has provided genetical and clinical evidence that they should be regarded as multidimensional in character.

The line of distinction between the highly prevalent "neurotic" forms of depression and the anxiety states is widely regarded as particularly unclear. Continuum concepts of depressive states are not easily reconciled with the existence of clear lines of demarcation anywhere in the entire territory that extends from the endogenous and psychotic depressions at one extreme to the anxiety neuroses and the disorders closely related to them at the other. In the light of the existing evidence, it would appear inconsistent to uphold a continuum or dimensional model of depression, while accepting that beyond some dividing line within the neurotic disorders a typological approach was the appropriate one.

A unitary theory of affective disorders, recognizing many variants merging insensibly with each other, was proposed forty years ago by Lewis (1934). He included anxiety neuroses, depressions with or without mania, severe or mild, and forms of disorder dominated by depersonalization or hypochrondiacal features as variants of a single manic-depressive illness. This was not so much a theory or model for the classification of affective illness as a denial that any classification of these disorders is possible. The view that holds that so many clinical syndromes blend imperceptibly with one another has no positive consequences. It can be neither substantiated nor refuted. It closes doors to the exploration of the possible causes for the differences between depressive states, with or without mania, endogenous depressions, and neurotic states, be the latter mainly anxious or hypochrondiacal. Clear hypotheses are precluded, for it is difficult to conceive of results that would be plainly inconsistent with such a model.

The modern form of theory differs from Lewis's unitary view in one main respect. Kendell (1968) takes the view that "there are important and fundamental differences between different depressions that are not simply differences in severity or chronicity." But he concludes that separate patient groups cannot be defined.

The foregoing will have made it clear why decades of inquiry and controversy have been directed toward resolution of this question. Some American observers, reviewing the history of the subject, have been inclined to conclude that the long-drawn-out debates as to whether distinct "endogenous" and "neurotic" patient groups (or identical distinctions by other names) existed were all "sound and fury signifying nothing." But it is accepted that this particular distinction must come prior to all others, and the evidence for this view has been outlined. The answer to the question posed is of far-reaching importance for the classification of all disorders of affect, the largest single group of psychiatric disorders encountered in hospital and community practice. In the next section the evidence bearing on this problem is, therefore, reviewed to ascertain whether such categorical or "continuum" concepts of depressive disorders are upheld by the results of inquiries that have made use of modern statistical techniques.

Studies with the Aid of Factor Analysis or Principle Component Analysis. The results of a large number of studies undertaken with the aid of factor analysis and related techniques have been discussed in numerous publications, and no comprehensive review will be attempted.

The issues under consideration are clarified by the conclusion of Mendels and Cochrane (1968), who reviewed seven factor analytic studies (Hamilton and White 1959; Kiloh and Garside 1963; Carney, Roth, and Garside 1965; Hordern 1965; Rosenthal and Klerman 1966; Rosenthal and Gudeman 1967; Mendels and Cochrane 1971). The most important finding to emerge from their comparative study was the wide measure of agreement reflected by the results of the independent groups of investigators. As Mendels and Cochrane point out, there was a "sufficient consensus" to support the independent status of the endogenous and reactive groups of disorders. One common pattern in these studies has been the extraction of a first general factor with positive loadings on all features (and therefore measuring severity) and a second factor, often bipolar and representing the antithesis of endogenous versus neurotic depression. The existence of at least two qualitatively different forms of depression is supported by the findings of other groups of workers, such as Fahy, Brandon, and Garside (1969) and Kay et al. (1969), and also by the observations of Kendell, whose data yielded an important "psychotic-neurotic" bipolar factor similar to what emerged from a number of different studies by Newcastle workers. In fact, the view advanced by Lewis (1934) and Mapother (1926)—that the main differences to be found in the field of affective disorders were entirely to be explained in terms of variation in severity or chronicity—is now rejected by most workers, although Hill (1968) appears to favor it.

The only question that continues to be subject to disagreement is whether distinct *patient groups* can be differentiated or whether there is so much overlap among them that most cases can not be allocated to one or the other of the syndromes as they combine elements of both. To decide whether patients can be separated into distinct groups, the distribution of their scores along a factor or dimension that differentiates between the syndromes can be plotted. If this proves to be continuous but is signifcantly non-normal and exhibits two or more modes, one is likely to be dealing with separate groups of depressed patients.

Distinct or Confluent Patient Groups. Although many groups of workers, notwithstanding differences in the patient populations studied, in sampling methods, and in techniques of assessment, have identified a bipolar "endogenous-neurotic" factor, not many have plotted their patients' scores on this factor to ascertain whether the distributions have been placed on record. A comparison of the results from the various centers reveals some differences, but the balance of the evidence favors the existence of distinct groups of depressive illness and is against the continuum hypothesis. Carney, Roth, and Garside (1965) obtained a bimodal distribution of summated scores, which made possible the allocation of approximately 85 percent of patients to one diagnostic group or other, leaving 15 percent unclassified (see fig. 6.1).

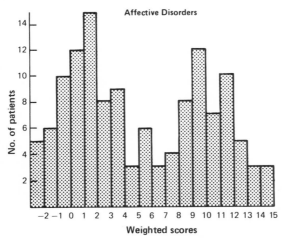

Figure 6.1. Distribution of weighted diagnostic scores on the Newcastle Depressive Scale in 129 patients with depression.

Similar results were obtained by Sandifer, Wilson, and Green (1966) and by Garside et al. (1971). The clear separation achieved in these studies could have arisen from the biased character of the samples of hospital inpatients studied. But such explanations were excluded by the observation of Fahy, Brandon, and Garside (1969) on a sample of patients with depression drawn from general practice. They obtained a bimodal distribution along a dimension of which distinct quality and unvarying nature of the depression had high positive loadings and which could be regarded as an endogenous depressive factor.

The observations of some other workers led them to different conclusions. Rosenthal (1967), finding a bimodal distribution of factors in the course of a study of depressed women, concluded that in most patients a mixture of syndromes was present. Paykel (1971) investigated varied sample of 220 patients with a number of rating scales and conducted a principal components analysis of thirty-five variables. The second bipolar factor again contrasted the patterns of neurotic and endogenous depression with high positive loading on such features as irritability, initial insomnia, depersonalization, somatic anxiety, obsessional symptoms, and negative loadings on age, loss of insight, retardation, distinct quality, diurnal variation with morning worsening. The distribution of scores on this factor showed on bimodality.

Kendell (1968a) has also published distributions that he construed as unimodal. Further, the explanation he advances for the discrepant results of the Newcastle group is that they are the product of clinical preconceptions about the classification of depression and the halo effects that issue from them. This would be valid and substantial if evidence controverting it had not been available from a source without bias favoring the existence of distinct patient groups. But some of Kendell's own findings are at variance with his conclusions. As Garside et al. (1971) have pointed out, one of the distributions Kendell has placed on record, namely that derived from the scores of 384 patients in his group B, departs significantly from normality ($x^2 = 52.0$, Df = 17, p 0.001).

Further evidence pointing in the same direction has recently come to light. Garside (1973) added some data derived by Kendell (1968 b), with the aid of the Newcastle Depressive Scale, to comparable data derived by Post (1972) from a group of depressed elderly patients. He obtained a significantly nonnormal and non-unimodal distribution of the scores of the resulting 222 patients.

Kendell and Post (1973) then added a further forty-nine scores and obtained a trimodal distribution, which they declared to be devoid of clinical meaning. Such a conclusion is untenable. The hypothesis that the clinical features of the depressive states are distributed on a continuum stands rejected by observations from an unbiased source. Moreover, as Figure 6.2 makes clear, the distributions derived from elderly and younger groups of patients are closely similar in shape. And far from being uninterpretable, the inflection at the score of five in both curves occurs at a point identical with the one that represented the line of cleavage between neurotic and endogenous depressions in curves published by Carney, Roth, and Garside (fig. 6.1). It therefore has a clear clinical significance. The second inflection in the curve can also be interpreted and proves consistent with another body of observations (Roth et al. 1972). For according to Post's own description, the elderly patients beyond this point exhibit prominent anxiety and somatic complaints without overt depression. They relate to another possible subdivision within the affective disorders, to be discussed at a later stage.

But even where indubitably normal distribution curves are obtained, the view that the phenomena they depict blend imperceptibly and that underlying discontinuities are excluded is logically untenable.

Some Theoretical Issues. A number of questions have been raised on theoretical grounds about the validity of inferences made from discontinuous curves, such as those derived from principle components analysis and related techniques. They are fully discussed elsewhere (Garside and Roth 1977), and only the more important can be briefly touched upon. Maxwell (1971) has expressed the view that the features submitted to factor analysis must be

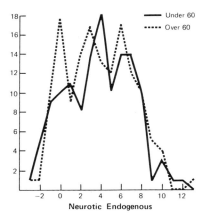

Figure 6.2. Distribution of weighted diagnostic scores on Newcastle Depressive Scale for elderly and younger groups of patients.

bivariate normal in distribution and that the populations studied must be homogenous. Discontinuous and bimodal distributions are therefore suspect and, as such, not interpretable. But this view is not shared by a number of other authorities, such as Cattell (1965) and Rummel (1970), and its application in practice yields some anomalous results.

Maxwell also holds that it is only the relationship between features, and not the grouping of the individuals who exhibit them, that can be investigated by factor analysis. This criticism has been voiced in many quarters (Kendell 1968). But it conflicts with the position adopted by other authorities. In particular, Gower (1966) has shown that with binary (0.1) data, which are the manner in which psychiatric observations are often expressed, principle components analysis is the statistical obverse of the clustering technique, numerical taxonomy. It follows that it can be legitimately employed in attempts to classify individuals as well as the features they exhibit.

The criticisms expressed by Eysenck (1970) concerning the inferences drawn in these controversies from bipolar factors and bimodal distributions misconceive the nature of the problems at issue in certain ways. Of course, scores on all components would be needed to depict patients as fully as possible from the information made available by the analysis. But it would be possible to build up a classification empirically along such lines. The objective in most inquiries has been the more limited and specific one of putting to the test hypotheses regarding the grouping of patients derived from clinical observations. Given certain limited and reasonable assumptions, the shape of the distribution along a bipolar component can be validly employed to submit a binary hypothesis regarding the depressive or any other group of disorders to critical tests.

For, as Moran (1966) has pointed out, there is no immaculate mathematical solution for the problem of finding a discriminating function that will demonstrate the existence of two different groups. Hence, "hit or miss" methods have to be used. Plotting the distribution on some relevant dimension derived from principle components analysis provides just such a method. An element of circularity is always inherent in the inferences drawn. Independent evidence to validate or refute the distinction arrived at from phenomenological data should, therefore, always be sought. Outcome and response to treatment provide appropriate tests for this purpose, and their contribution as validating criteria in the classification of depression is briefly discussed in the next section.

The Evidence from Outcome and Response to Treatment. The value of any system of classification has to be assessed from its ability to make predictions not anticpated from its defining terms. Both the bipolar-unipolar and the endogenous-neurotic dichotomy receive some validation from the prognostic judgments made possible by diagnosis. Only the salient points from a large body of evidence can be considered within the scope of this paper. Endogenous depressions prove to have a better outcome and a superior response to most forms of treatment of proven efficacy, as in general—though not in all cases—it is the endogenous patients that have the more severe illness. A difference in the opposite direction would have been expected if the syndromes were separated by severity alone.

In recent years clinical trials have shown tricyclic compounds to be effective in the treatment of "neurotic" depression (Klerman et al. 1974; Parkel et al. 1975). These findings are not in conflict with the results from the earlier comparative studies of Kiloh, Ball, and Garside (1962), which showed that the results achieved in endogenous cases are superior. A similar divergence is evident in the therapeutic effects of electroconvulsive treatment (ECT). Indeed, in endogenous cases with psychotic features, such as depressive delusions and hallucinations, pharmacotherapy is ineffective while ECT usually elicits a prompt response. In neurotic depressions, convulsive therapy is significantly less effective than in endogenous illnesses (Carney, Roth, and Garside 1965). And although in severely ill and actively suicidal patients ECT may have to be employed, it is advisable to keep the number of treatments down to a minimum and to avoid it, in this group, as far as possible. The fact that in individual experiments it has proved possible to provide a better prediction of outcome directly from clinical features than from diagnosis (Carney, Roth, and Garside 1965), is not surprising, given the multiplicity of factors that shape outcome. The significant point is that, notwithstanding these many influences, predictions that apply generally and have a substantial measure of reliability can be made on the basis of diagnosis alone.

The pattern of response to behavioral therapies that have been recently introduced in the treatment of depression is just the opposite of that described in relation to electroconvulsive therapy. Among treatments derived from learning theory, reinforcement of active and assertive behavior and selective inattention to depressive conduct have been applied. Favorable results have been described in neurotic depressions (Wolpe 1971; Lazarus 1968). But psychotic forms of depression fail to respond.

Suggestions for Diagnostic Decision Making in the Uncertain Areas Between Depressive Syndromes. There is general agreement that, while the polar extremes of the syndromes are easily recognized, there is an indeterminate area between them made up of a group of patients in whom diagnosis is difficult because the disorders present features of both conditions. In fact, Kendell (1968) accepts that there are qualitatively distinct forms of depressive illness. The continuum view is justified by the fact that the proportion of patients who exhibit a mixed picture is so high that most cases cannot be unequivocally assigned to one group or the other.

But some present less difficulty in diagnosis than others. For in the area of overlap there are at least two populations of patients. In the first the clinical features are vague, neither clinical profile figuring in a recognizable form. In the second group a clearly delineated endogenous or psychotic syndrome is found in the setting of a number of prominent neurotic symptoms, both depressive and anxious. In this latter group a diagnosis of endogenous depression is appropriate for two reasons. It is implicit in the classificatory schemes that stem from Kraepelin that endogenous and psychotic states command precedence in diagnosis over neurotic ones, just as indubitable schizophrenic syndromes are given priority in diagnosis in the presence of associated affective disturbances, irrespective of their form or severity. Second, it is endogenous syndromes that govern decisions relating to treatment, prognosis, and outcome of the presenting illness.

On the basis of such a division the indeterminate area between depressions could be substantially reduced. But it rests at present on clinical reasoning and observation, and its validity has to be exposed to further tests.

Subdivisions of the "Endogenous" and "Neurotic" Depression

Good classifications are simple and parsimonious. They establish the smallest possible number of classes required to subsume in an inclusive, comprehensive, and logical manner the phenomena under examination. This is merely a restatement of Occam's razor. There are, however, certain subdivisions of each of the two main depressive groups that have achieved recognition or have begun to gain acceptance through their repeated replication in the observations of different workers. The division of the endogenous group into unipolar and bipolar groups is now generally accepted, and only a few additional points need to be made. In most studies of the endogenous and neurotic problem, the former category included both groups. But bipolar cases in the Newcastle studies, for example, made up 10 percent or less of the total, and the phenomenology of this form of depression could not be systematically studied. Recurrent mania originally classed as "monopolar" by Leonhard is now recognized as having affinities with bipolar disorders. "Mixed" psychoses in Kraepelin's sense deserve brief mention, in that this rare confluence of manic and depressive features is liable to make an incongrous impression and to elicit an erroneous diagnosis of schizophrenia.

But it is in the "neurotic" group of depressions that there is the greatest need for improvements in classification and for more clear and specific indications for pharmacological treatment. This broad category constitutes the largest single group among the affective disorders. There are few generally accepted landmarks. But findings from different centers have in recent years shown a substantial measure of consistency. (These are reviewed in the next section.)

The main features are a depressive mood change whose severity fluctuates with change in circumstance, initial insomnia, lack of consistent diurnal variation, irritability, prominent anxiety, adverse life situation in more or less intimate association with the onset of symptoms, and an unstable personality setting of varying character.

Neurotic Depressive Syndromes Derived from Multivariate Analyses. Recent investigations making use of multivariate analyses of clinical findings have shed new light on the classification of this group of disorders but have also posed some difficult problems. Paykel (1971) applied a cluster analytic technique to 165 subjects drawn from his original 220-patient sample. The first cluster corresponded in its features to the classical picture of psychotic depression with retardation, delusions of guilt, anorexia, delayed insomnia, and low scores for total stress. This was the oldest group. The second group was middle-aged, and the patients were described as "anxious depressives." They scored high on anxiety, obsessional symptoms, depersonalization, and fatigue and had a high incidence of previous depressive episodes and high neuroticism scores with only moderate depression. The remaining two groups were younger and not very clearly differentiated. One scored high on hostility and "self-pity," and the last group showed a mild illness with marked mood fluctuation in the setting of personality disorder.

The "self-pitying constellation" recurs in the descriptions from a number of different studies. It refers to a tendency to cast blame on others and on the environment, together with self-commiseration and demanding behavior. A similar personality setting is depicted in the descriptions of Rosenthal and Gudeman (1967). The second and third syndromes are recognizable in the findings of Fahy, Brandon, and Garside (1969); and all three groups, together with the endogenous syndrome, figure in the observations published by Kiloh et al. (1972). The "hostile" group is recognizable again in the histrionic, aggressive, and manipulative behavior of the patients of Lazare and Klerman (1968) and in the "hysteroid dysphoria" of Klein and Daves (1969). Kiloh et al. concluded that reactive depression is composed of several groups merging by small gradations into one another, the whole class constituting a continuum or a dimensional entity in contrast to the categorical nature of endogenous depression.

Certain points arise. Despite the fact that several of the observers have concluded that the different syndromes form a continuum, they lapse into unmistakably categorical language when depicting them. Such terms as "hostile" depression are gaining currency, although the reliability of such a clinical diagnosis is not clearly established. There also are certain assumptions needing validation, in the use of such concepts as "hostility," "self-pity," and "hysterical dysphoria." For they implicitly use *personality diagnosis* to help characterize *depressive illness*. If this can be shown to assist discrimination and prediction, personality features need to be systematically explored, appropriate measures applied, and a separate personality diagnosis entered explicitly for all groups including bipolar and unipolar endogenous depressions.

Until further observations have accumulated, certain qualifications are needed as far as the practical application of these concepts is concerned. Clinical observations teach that personality features and illness syndromes vary independently of one another to a considerable extent. Some severe and seriously suicidal endogenous depressive disorders present in the setting of a hysterical personality, the features of which are accentuated by the emotional disturbances. They often respond in a prompt and favorable manner to physical treatment. Though predominantly young, such patients are to be found in all age groups. The histrionic and demanding conduct may be no more than a pathoplastic coloring lent to the presenting illness. On the other hand, among the aged it is not rare to find stable personalities with low neuroticism scores who break down de novo in the face of stress. They may need protection from a diagnosis of endogenous depression, which is too readily assumed, for they fare badly with the treatments that follow. It may be concluded, in this section, that the subdivision of neurotic depressions that emerges from the findings of Paykel and of Kiloh et al. may be tentatively accepted. But their application in clinical practice should be cautious as well as tentative for the reasons stated and also because the reliability of the personality diagnoses used and their role in the classification of depression requires further investigation.

Anxiety and Phobic Features and Neurotic Depression. A further point is raised by the prominence of somatic and psychic anxiety in the neurotic group of depressions. Investigations ostensibly confined to classifications of depressive illness have, on statistical analysis, repeatedly isolated symptom clusters and patient groups that appear to have clear affinities to the anxiety states. The studies of Fahy, Bandon, and Garside (1969) in general practice are a case in point. One hundred twenty-six patients diagnosed as suffering from a depressive illness were studied. One group of patients identified by the factorial analysis proved to have diffuse anxiety, situational phobias, and panic attacks. The phobic features are prone to elude detection unless specifically inquired after. In the study of Hordern et al. (1965) a cluster of anxiety features exhibiting little association with depressive symptoms and an adverse treatment response was identified. Patients with severe and incapacitating phobic symptoms or somatic anxiety are liable at some stages of illness to develop severe sustained and, at times, suicidal depressive symptoms. There are no clear guidelines or rules for arriving at a diagnosis in such cases.

The question posed is whether the depressive illnesses and neurotic depressions in particular are clearly demarcated from anxiety neuroses. If depressions have to be depicted in dimensional terms, as Kendell (1968) believes, they should merge imperceptibly with the anxiety neuroses and related neurotic states. However, investigations that have been conducted to test this continuum hypothesis have not upheld it; these issues are considered in the section that follows.

Depression in Relation to Anxiety States and Other Neurotic Disorders

Depressive illnesses, whether endogenous or neurotic, frequently have a coloring of anxiety, agitation, and fear-laden preoccupation with unlikely dangers. The autonomic disturbances we associate with anxiety, namely tachycardia, excessive perspiration, tremor, and gastrointestinal disturbance, are also frequently present. Conversely, in states of anxiety—particularly those that endure for considerable periods—depression, helplessness, and pessimism often supervene. The association of such symptoms does not signify that the syndromes to which their name has become attached are indistinguishable from one another. Depression of affect may be found in schizophrenia, paranoid states, obsessional phobic and hysterical neuroses, and such organic states as epilepsy and cerebro-vascular disease, the last often associated with a substantial suicidal risk. But this ubiquity of depression does not call into question the existence of discrete and independent depressive syndromes.

However, such concepts as "anxious" depression and "secondary" depression in anxiety states make it clear that landmarks are indistinct in this area. They also serve as a reminder that, despite our confident use of them, terms such as "anxiety" and "depression" are not very precise. More clear delineation of the clinical disorders in which these affects are predominant may also help provide a more exact and objective definable referent for them. But as the discussion in the foregoing section implies, difficulties in the classification of depressive disorders arise in considerable measure from ambiguities concerning their relationship with anxiety states. These are not resolved by ad hoc concepts, such as "secondary depression" (Feighner et al. 1972) for ambiguous forms of affective disorders. The question is whether anxiety and depressive syndromes can be clearly differentiated or whether they merge insensibly with one another. The observations carried out in this area, together with some new findings, have been reviewed in a number of papers (Gurney et al. 1972; Roth et al. 1972; Roth, 1976a; Roth et al. 1976), which should be consulted for details. Here a brief summary will be presented.

Four main lines of evidence emerged from these inquiries:

a) *Phenomenological findings.* Clinical obervations recorded in the course of structured interviews from 145 patients were submitted to principle components and discriminant function analysis. From these studies a diagnostic index (table 6.1) was developed, which made it possible to achieve clear separation with a small amount of overlap between patients with anxiety states on the one hand and those with depressive illness on the other. It will be seen that the symptoms highly correlated with a diagnosis of anxiety included panic attacks (accompanied in many cases by severe autonomic disturbance and sometimes syncope), situational phobias, severe and persistent (as distinct from intermittent) anxiety symptoms, derealization, a close association with physical illness at onset, prominent neurotic traits in childhood, and marked emotional dependence.

Among the depressive features were a persistently depressed mood, early wakening, suicidal tendencies, retardation, and a low neuroticism score on the Maudsley personality inventory (MPI). The separation achieved with the principle components analysis was confirmed by means of a cluster analysis. And recently a second sample of cases with anxiety states and depressive disorder, but excluding endogenous depression, provided confirmatory evidence that a relatively clear line of demarcation between anxiety and depressive syndromes should be possible (Monjoy and Roth, unpublished observations; Roth, 1976a).

b) *Follow-up studies* by independent observers (Kerr et al. 1972) validated the distinctions made in the course of the initial clinical investigations. Throughout the forty-two-month period covered by the follow-up inquiries, there was a higher proportion of improved patients among the depressed than among the anxious patients, and the differences were statistically significant. The two groups were found to have differed significantly both in respect to the treatments that had been prescribed for them independently by consultants unconnected with the inquiry and in respect to the response

Table 6.1.
Diagnostic anxiety/depression index derived from
discriminate function analysis of clinical item components

Item		*Score*	
Neurotic traits in childhood	3 or more	+	10
	2 or less	+	5
	none		0
Dependence	present	+	6
	absent		0
Physical stress	severe	+	16
	mild/moderate	+	8
	none		0
Panic attacks	3 or more per week	+	20
	2 or less per week	+	10
	none		0
Situational phobias	marked	+	6
	mild/moderate	+	3
	none		0
Derealization	marked &/or persistent	+	2
	mild	+	1
	none		0
Anxiety symptoms	6 or more	+	12
	3 to 5	+	6
	less than 3		0
Depressed mood	severe	−	18
	mild/moderate	−	9
	none		0
Early waking	present	−	4
	absent		0
Suicidal tendencies	attempt	−	12
	ideas	−	6
	none		0
Retardation	present	−	6
	absent		0
Obsessional symptoms	marked	+	4
	mild	+	2
	none		0
Neurotic (MPI)	0- 8	−	15
	9-16	−	12
	17-24	−	9
	25-32	−	6
	33-40	−	3
	41-48		0

Ranges

Anxiety range	11	78
Doubtful range	3	10
Depressive range	55	2

Martin Roth

Table 6.2.
Response to treatment on discharge and at six months

Treatment		Improved N (%)		
		Total group	Anxiety states	Depressive illness
ECT				
N	. . .	42	9	28 . . . .
Discharge	. . .	28 (66.7)	2 (22.2)	24 (85.7)*
Six months	. . .	27 (64.3)	2 (22.2)	21 (75.0)†
Tricyclic drugs				
N	. . .	56	18	27 . . . .
Discharge	. . .	35 (62.5)	5 (27.8)	23 (85.2)*
Six months	. . .	32 (57.1)	5 (27.8)	21 (77.8)†
Monoamine oxidase inhibitors				
N	. . .	44	37	7 . . . .
Discharge	. . .	29 (65.9)	25 (67.6)	4 (57.1)
Six months	. . .	24 (54.5)	20 (54.1)	4 (57.1)

Source: From Gurney et al. *Brit. J. Psychiat.* 117: 251-55, 1970.

† = p 0.05
* = p 0.01

they made to ECT and tricyclic antidepressants (Gurney et al. 1970). The outcome in depressed patients had been superior in respect to both treatments. As will be seen in Table 6.2, ECT and tricyclic compounds elicited significantly superior results in depressive illness to those in patients with anxiety states (who had frequently received a diagnosis of depressive disorder from consultants in charge). No such differences were obtained in the case of MAOI substances. But the number of depressions so treated was small. It is of interest that the follow-up revealed a significant increase in mortality over normal expectation; this study was confined to men in the simple anxiety state and neurotic depression groups (table 6.3).

c) There was *little cross-over* in pattern of illness displayed during the relapse that occurred in the follow-up period. When they relapsed, the patients with anxiety neurosis and those with depressive disorder tended to exhibit syndromes similar to those they had presented at the time of the first examination.

d) The clinical *features that best predicted outcome* in anxiety states proved to be different from the best predictors in the depressions, and there was little overlap (Schapira et al. 1972; Kerr, Roth, and Schapira 1974). This finding was more consistent with two distinct forms of illness than with disorders that merged with each other.

Table 6.3.
Observed and expected mortality rates of the diagnostic groups

Diagnostic group	No. of patients	All deaths			Death excluding suicides		
		Mortality		Level of significance	Mortality		Level of significance
		Expected	Observed		Expected	Observed	
Males							
Agoraphobic and related states	12	0.120	1	n.s.	0.120	0	....
Simple anxiety state	16	0.377	4	p=0.0008	0.339	3	p=0.0055
Neurotic depression	14	1.180	4	p=0.034	1.180	4	0=0.034
Endogenous depression	14	1.465	4	n.s.	1.403	3	n.s.
Total depressed group	28	2.636	8	p=0.0057	2.574	7	p=0.016
Females							
Agoraphobic and related states	28	0.185	0	....	....	0	....
Simple anxiety state	16	0.143	0	....	....	0	....
Neurotic depression	17	0.443	2	n.s.	0.443	2	n.s.
Endogenous depression	11	0.373	0	....	....	0	....
Total depressed group	28	0.820	2	n.s.	0.820	2	n.s.

Figure 6.3 shows the diagnostic index derived from principle components analysis of fifty-eight clinical items. This was followed by a discriminant function analysis using those patients in whom a diagnosis could be made with some confidence. When patients' scores on this index were plotted, the distribution showed a clear separation of anxiety and depression groups (Gurney el al. 1972) (figure 6.3). A canonical variate analysis undertaken to achieve maximal separation between four hypothetical patient groups on fifty eight variables provided further information for purposes of classification. To depict the patients' scores on all variates would require more than two dimensions in space. Figure 6.4 shows distribution of variate I alone and is intended to be schematic. Endogenous depressions (unipolar-bipolar depressions) fall at the left extreme and are wholly separated from the other groups. Neurotic depressions, anxiety states, and agoraphobic and related neuroses show some measure of overlap, but they occupy distinct and separate parts of the distribution. Further reference is made to this figure at a later stage.

On the basis of investigations similar to those described under *a* above, diagnostic index was devised that served also to separate phobic states (which were almost entirely agoraphobic and social phobic neuroses) from simple anxiety states (Burney and Roth, unpublished observations). In the case of other phobic neuroses and obsessional states, each of which has some affinities with anxiety neurosis, formal inquiries have not been undertaken. But clear distinctons are generally assumed in clinical practice and are in part validated by differences in outcome and, to some extent, by the differential effects of behavior therapy and psychotropic drugs in agoraphobia and social

AFFECTIVE SURVEY
PATIENT SCORES ON REGRESSION SCALE

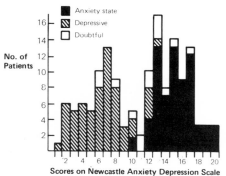

Figure 6.3. Patient scores on anxiety/depression index regression scale.

phobia in anxiety states with solitary circumscribed phobic (or obsessional) features and obsessive-compulsive states proper. More systematic investigations of the relationships between classification and treatment response are needed in this area.

Some brief comments are needed to serve as a bridge between the present section and the one that follows. Little attention has been given in taxonomic studies to the longitudinal perspective the degree of consistency and of change observed in individuals in respect of the clincal disorders with which they present over long stretches of time. There is little factual information to work from. Attention has already been drawn to the fact that over three- to four-year periods of observation, cross-overs from one type of disorder to a wholly different one are relatively rare. However, over longer periods one form of transformation is occasionally seen, and it is of considerable theoretical as well as practical importance. In a comparative study of schizophreniform and "process" types of schizophrenic disorder in Newcastle (McClelland et al. 1966) patients in the former group were found, in a proportion of cases, to have presented some years previously with a typical, fully documented anxiety or other neurotic illness. The transition had often been preceded by stress of exceptionally severe nature or stress in close association with physical illness. In some cases a psychosis is the first illness to present, although the premorbid personality will have exhibited conspicuous neurotic traits or

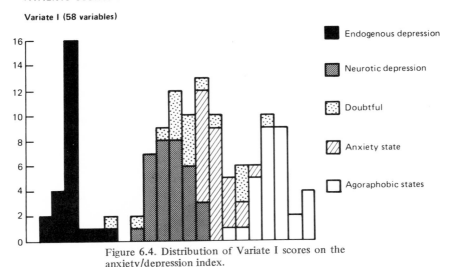

PATIENTS' SCORES ON VARIABLE 1

Variate I (58 variables)

Figure 6.4. Distribution of Variate I scores on the anxiety/depression index.

other evidence of emotional vulnerability. These patients constitute one among several links with the next subject, schizophreniform disorders.

Affective Disorder and the Schizophreniform Group of Illness

Several developments have made it plain that any discussion of diagnosis of the classification and general theory of depressive states would be incomplete if it failed to take account of the poorly charted borderland between the affective disorders and schizophrenia. One relevant line of evidence comes from the Danish-American studies of mental illness in the biological and adoptive families of adopted schizophrenics (Kety et al. 1968). While the families of chronic and borderline schizophrenics were found to have a significant excess of individuals with schizophrenia or borderline forms of it, no such hereditary link was found in cases of acute schizophrenia.

A substantial proportion of acute cases has a certain affinity with the affective disorders. A coloring of depression and anxiety tends to be prominent and often causes diagnostic difficulties. This feature has played an important part in generating the concept of schizoaffective psychosis (Kasanin 1933). The second link is constituted by the impressive psychological and temporal association between stress, often of a severe and overwhelming nature, and the onset of psychotic symptoms. The detailed phenomenological studies of Labhardt (1963) and the Swiss School exemplify in a particularly clear manner the problems posed by the entire group of disorders. The emotional traumas and physical illness at onset were onerous or life-threatening in character, and the symptomatology covered a wide range of features, including paranoid, hallucinatory, and catatonic symptoms, transient clouding of consciousness, anxiety with severe vegetative disturbance, agitation, and some hysterical symptoms. But the families are almost completely free of schizophrenic hereditary taint. The response to treatment was prompt and favorable with no postschizophrenic sequelae. The Newcastle studies (McClelland et al. 1968) pointed in a similar direction. A discriminant function analysis showed that 132 cases of schizophrenia of "process" type were differentiated from schizophreniform illness, not by "nuclear" features, but by the presence of neurotic personality traits, attention seeking, emotional and variable clouding in acute stages.

A third link with affective disorder was established by the observations of Scandinavian authors, who have for some decades attached great importance to the psychogenic and schizophreniform disorders (Langfeldt 1956; Strömgren 1968). Some figures provided by Strömgren make it clear that a relatively high proportion of patients are allocated to these diagnostic groups in Denmark. In 1961 and 1962 some 22 percent of the total number of psychotics admitted to Danish psychiatric hospitals were diagnosed overall as suffering from "psychogenic psychoses." They were as large a group as schizophrenia and affective psychosis. Strömgren broadly accepts Schneider's classification of these cases in three groups: (1) *emotional reaction*, which may include stupor, psychotic depression, or mania, including the so-called "funeral mania"; (2) *disorders of consciousness*, assuming the form of clouded or delirious states; (3) *paranoid psychoses*. Scandinavian psychiatrists tend, on the whole, to utilize a painstaking phenomenological method in diagnosis and classification, and their approach conforms for the large part to the Kraepelinian system.

In the present context the findings of particular importance are those of Welner and Strömgren (1958). In their cases of psychogenic schizophreniform illness they describe a typical "nuclear" picture except for a well-preserved capacity for emotional contact and lack of autism. However, there was a raised prevalence of neuroses and character disorders among siblings but no increase in morbid risk for schizophrenia. The family studies of Clayton, Desmaris, and Winokur (1968) in thirty-nine patients with schizoaffective disorder also led them to conclude that they were dealing with a variant of affective illness. The findings in respect to heredity were, therefore, essentially in agreement with those reported by the Danish-American observers in relation to acute schizophrenia.

A fourth group of observations that serves as a connecting link is provided by the "cycloid" psychoses of Leonhard (1957), which have recently been the subject of a special inquiry by Perris (1974b). This author finds no evidence that the mixed symptomatology of this group is determined by a blend of schizophrenic and manic heredity. His findings tend to confirm those of Leonhard that families exhibit a high morbid risk for the same distinctive "homotypical" form of disorder rather than affective or typical schizophrenic psychosis for the same. However, his preliminary findings in relation to the effects of lithium carbonate in the treatment of this group of disorders show that the number of episodes of illness in a follow-up period of one to five years was reduced, in the most favorable group, from a mean of 2.06 episodes to 0.50 episodes, a highly significant result. And although half of the fifteen patients studied by Baastrup (1973) relapsed during the follow-up, his experience was not wholly at variance. The possibility that within the schizoaffective cases there may be a distinctive form of psychosis independent of the two main functional psychotic groups is not generally accepted. Florid manic or "mixed" affective psychoses, often dominated by paranoid symptomatology and passivity feelings or other isolated schizophrenic-like features, commonly cause difficulties in diagnosis. In the author's view these are often re-solved by long-term observation in favor of affective psychosis. At any rate, the possibility of an affinity between "cycloid" and bipolar illnesses does not appear to be refuted by the findings to date.

Most of the cases that have been discussed in this section are neatly classed with the affective disorders in the St. Louis group's scheme of classification by the application of two criteria of exclusion, attached to the diagnosis of schi-zophrenia; those with symptoms of less than six months' duration and those with a history of having had a previous manic or depressive illness fail to qualify (Feighner et al. 1972). This provides some useful guidelines for clini-cal purposes and discourages premature diagnoses of "schizophrenia." But the sharp demarcation thus drawn entails a circular argument, and its heuristic value is dubious. The possibility of discovering through comparative studies why schizophrenic syndromes prove evanescent in some cases and evolve into chronic disorders in others is precluded. The genetical differences between acute and chronic schizophrenia are also matters for investigation by com-parison rather than for artificial exclusion from the agenda of exploration.

This group of disorders figures prominently among the diagnoses made in some countries. For this reason, among others, all the forms discussed here should be included as contrast populations in inquiries into the classification and diagnosis of both affective disorder and schizophrenia; the evidence de-mands that they should be compared and contrasted with each group of dis-orders. As far as treatment is concerned, pharmacological therapy has to be decided empirically according to the features and associations of the indivi-dual case. A high proportion pursue a benign course, and long-acting pheno-thiazines are therefore contraindicated in the early stages of management. Patients should be accorded a diagnosis that places them into this "schizo-phreniform" group or be considered as possibly eligible for it under the fol-lowing conditions:

1. When previous attacks of illness have been indubitably manic or de-pressive in character.

2. When previous illnesses have presented in the form of a typical phobic or anxiety state. In subsequent relapse the form of the illness in such patients will often resume its erstwhile character.

3. When the onset of psychotic symptoms has followed closely upon, and in impressive association with, exceptionally severe or overwhelming psychological stress or grave physical illness.

4. In those cases of acute psychosis with some schizophrenic features in which the psychosis fails to remit or improve after more than six weeks of treatment with adequate doses of phenothiazines and a course of electro-

convulsive treatment, the possibility of an atypical manic variety of schizophreniform illness should always be considered in diagnosis. In many such
patients, prominent affective features will prompt review of the diagnosis
at an earlier stage.

5. When a blend of schizophrenic and conspicuous depressive or manic
symptomatology presents after psychological stress or physical illness or in
the setting of a neurotically unstable (rather than schizoid, paranoid, hostile,
or seclusive) personality. But when "schizoaffective" symptomatology
appears out of an entirely clear sky, the disorder should logically be classed
as schizophrenic. The latter illness should be accorded priority in diagnosis
unless circumstances or settings differ in the ways stipulated above.

A Tentative Classification of the Affective Disorders

A synthesis of the observations and concepts reviewed in this and the preceding paper will now be attempted so as to provide a tentative basis for a
classification of the affective disorders. Figure 6.5 represents the proposed
scheme in a diagrammatic form, which seeks to replicate the four stages in
the decision-making process that would be followed before arriving at a final
diagnosis. The categories chosen as alternatives for decision making at each
level have been derived to a large extent from the theoretical evidence summarized or referred to in this paper but are based in part on clinical
judgments that need to be tested. The scheme attempts a synthesis of older
taxonomic concepts, such as the endogenous-neurotic distinction, with those
that have gained recognition recently, such as the unipolar-bipolar differentiation.

The rubric *affective disorder* at the top (Level I) of the decision tree implies that the patient has been judged to suffer from a psychiatric illness as
distinct from "normal" affective response. The evidence that validates such a
distinction has been reviewed elsewhere (Roth 1976a, b).

At the next stage (Level II) the choice lies between an endogenous and a
neurotic form of affective disorder. These are depicted here as categorically
distinct. Although some measure of overlap indubitably obtains, the balance
of the evidence favors the view that the patient populations are separate and
that a clear diagnostic decision can be reached in the great majority of cases.

A recent reinvestigation of the findings recorded by Lewis's influential
paper of 1934 has a particular theory for subdivision at this level. For as
Lewis explicitly subsumed the disorders dominated by anxiety under the
heading of depressive states, his cases of "melancholia" would have been
drawn from disorders of affect as wide as that covered in this review and in

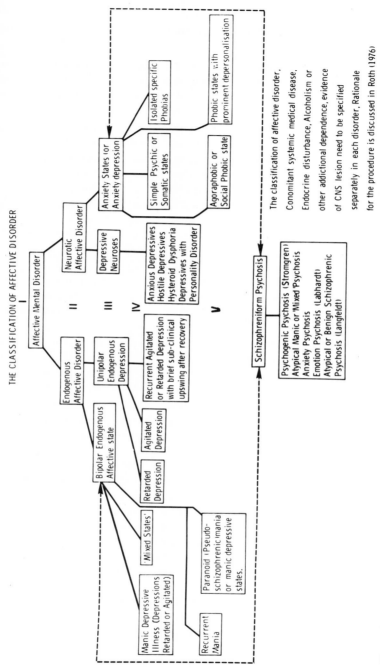

Figure 6.5. Diagrammatic representation of affective disorders classification scheme.

the classification under consideration here. His data were published in sufficient detail to enable Kiloh and Garside (1963) to submit them to a principle
components and cluster analysis. With each method the patients were
separated by their scores on the relevant dimensions into two clearly distinct
groups. The result was consistent with the separation proposed at this level
into all patients with endogenous disorders on the one hand and those with
neurotic illness, whether predominantly depressed or anxious, on the other.

There is general dissatisfaction that the terms "endogenous" and
"neurotic" may convey the impression that the disorder is merely one
episode isolated from a state of lifelong neuroticism. But neurotic affective
disorders commence at a certain point in time and have a course and outcome of their own. The terms are intended to depict, first, a specific clinical
syndrome and, second, a form of affective disturbance in which an orderly
and understandable relationship is generally found between premorbid personality features—together with its vulnerable points, the stresses that im-
pinge upon these Achilles heels—and the form of emotional disturbance that
follows. In "endogenous" illness, on the other hand, while adverse life situations may precede the onset of symptoms, the disorder that follows is dis-
proportionately severe, sustained, and difficult to comprehend in the light
of circumstances, and it pursues a relatively autonomous course unaffected
by life events.

At the next level (III) the endogenous cases shown on the left divide into
the unipolar and bipolar depressions. Leonhard may have been in error when
he confined his concept to the "endogenous psychoses." But nowhere has his
specific hypothesis been refuted. And there are sound reasons for limiting his
concept to the clinical territory for which he intended it and where it has
proved of heuristic value. The neurotic affective disorders at Level III sub-
divide into the depressive neuroses and the anxiety states, which could also
be appropriately named "anxiety depressions."

In both unipolar and bipolar groups there is a small proportion of patients
with nihilistic or other delusions, sometimes with hallucinations, loss of insight, and misinterpretation of reality. The suicidal risk is high, particularly
in agitated cases, but drug treatment is often ineffective by itself. For the
sake of simplicity in presentation, these small psychotic subgroups are not
shown separately.

At the fourth level the bipolar endogenous affective states may be subdivided into several groups. First come the depressions, which are predominantly retarded but may be agitated in picture. The next group comprises
recurrent mania, which is now generally recognized as having a kinship with
the bipolar rather than unipolar cases. Third comes a group of patients who

exhibit a blend of both manic and depressive features, or a "mixed" psychosis in Kraepelin's original sense. Finally, in a proportion of manic and mixed cases the picture is dominated by paranoid symptoms associated at times with ideas of influence and passivity. As elation and infectiousness of mood may not be in evidence, these patients are particularly prone to be diagnosed as schizophrenic. As the same picture of a florid, seemingly paranoid psychosis may present consistently in the same case, this group deserves separate mention.

Unipolar endogenous cases are often described as being unusually agitated. But they may be retarded. The third group of unipolar cases at Level IV with "brief sub-clinical unswings" of mood after recovery are mentioned separately because they raise problems in diagnosis.

The depressive neuroses at Level IV are divisible into the four distinct subgroups shown, which have already been discussed. It is nothworthy that the subdivisions proposed on the basis of multivariate analyses by Paykel (1971), Kiloh et al. (1972), and others, were a more elaborate and precise version of distinctions already made by Gillespie (1929), who divided his "reactive depressions" into psychoneurotic depression and depressions in constitutional psychopaths. He therefore recognized that the premorbid personality setting contributed substantially to the differentiation between groups. "Hostile depression" and "hysteroid dysphoria" may refer to this same syndrome, but it is uncertain at present whether this is the case. The anxiety neuroses at Level IV can be subdivided into (1) simple anxiety states, which are predominantly somatic or psychic but often exhibit a blend of both kinds of symptomatology, (2) agoraphobic and social phobic neuroses, and (3) phobic states with prominent depersonalization and isolated specific phobias. Of the latter, animal phobias and their isolated phobic symptoms, which are readily circumvented, are of little importance. This is not true of illness phobias, which are among the features of anxiety states that occur in the setting of obsessional personality traits; such patients fluctuate between doubt and delusion about the possibility of cancer or fatal illness. Episodes of severe depression with serious suicidal risk may require urgent treatment. A clear dividing line has been demonstrated, with the aid of multivariate analyses (Gurney and Roth, unpublished observations), between simple anxiety states and disabling forms of phobic neurosis (excluding isolated specific phobias), and there are some parallel differences in pattern of outcome.

A proportion of cases of anxiety and phobic states pursue a chronic or fluctuating course and present in some phases with profound depressive symptoms. The depression in these cases evolves in a manner that is reminiscent of progression from anxiety to depression in the accounts of "deprivation" neuroses given by ethologists and of Seligman's description of "learned helplessness," to which further reference is made at a time by depression and despair and, unless specific questions are asked, phobic symptoms and even a housebound state of long duration may fail to come to light. Yet these core features have a significant bearing upon the treatment indicated and the ultimate prognosis. The appropriate diagnosis is that of the primary disorder, namely anxiety or phobic neurosis.

The lines drawn in Figure 6.5 between groups of affective disorder and the schizophreniform category shown below are tentative and are intended to indicate the best known associations, which are not necessarily the only ones. The main groups are definable at present among those cases related to the affective disorders. In the "emotion" psychoses of Labhardt the prominence of an affect of anxiety and terror, the overwhelming forms of stress, and the autonomic disturbance suggest an affinity with states of anxiety rather than depression. This appears also to be true of some other schizophreniform disorders with the course and characteristics of a "psychogenic" state. For prior to the onerous "key event" that ushers in the illness, many such patients are only oversensitive and anxious, but a social phobic state or other anxiety neurosis of disabling severity can often be defined. The transition from this neurosis to a paranoid state of psychosis can be observed propsectively in a proportion of cases in clinical practice. In contrast to these cases with affinities to anxiety states are the florid psychoses diagnosed as schizophrenic in one or more attacks but judged after a longer period of observation to be atypical manic or bipolar psychoses. The connecting lines between schizophreniform disorders and Level III, therefore, end at anxiety states and bipolar disorders.

The interrupted lines are meant to indicate that schizophreniform illnesses are not within the exclusive domain of the affective disorders above, and the direction of the arrows shows that the form in which the disorder presents may shift from the "schizophreniform" to the "typical" affective form or vice versa over long periods of observation.

The note at the bottom of Figure 6.5 suggests that associated systemic medical disease, alcoholism, and other disorders should be stipulated separately in each disorder. The justification for depicting associated illness in this manner and the problems associated with the primary-secondary concept formulated by the St. Louis group have been discussed in the first paper. The relationship between this classification and response to treatment has been discussed in the first paper and in other publications (Gurney et al. 1970; Roth et al. 1976).

Classification and Models of Depression

This review of the problems of classification has necessarily focused on a restricted range of observations—those bearing upon the phenomenology and classification of disorders of affect. A narrowly confined theoretical discourse such as this may seem remote from the holistic approach of Adolf Meyer and the model of illness implicit in it. The biological model used in taxonomic and related studies may at times seem so abstract that it is removed from the sufferings of the individuals it purports to depict with precision. But different models serve different purposes; the distance is more apparent than real. Engaged in the care of patients, the properly trained psychiatrist has learned from the contributions of Freud and Meyer to examine the familial setting, the social background, and the psychological influences that have emanated from the past and the present. But now, clear or testable hypotheses for scientific purposes can emerge from individuals conceived of as unique and require fomulation from every possible angle that could possibly prove helpful in mitigation of their plight.

The fact of the matter is that the models needed for the purposes of clinical practice on the one hand and for solving problems of advancing knowledge of psychiatry on the other are different. The first require a wide range of observations from different disciplines; everything that can serve comprehensively to depict the individual or to mobilize help for him. But for the second, the need is for defining features of the greatest generality that will serve to place the individual in a class. Even when making formulations about ostensibly "unique" patients, those who draw upon Meyerian or psychodynamic teaching must be drawing upon models or group profiles they have unconsciously assembled in the course of experience. Without such models, statements about individual patients would have been random, idiosyncratic, and worthless. About the really unique they would not have had anything to say. This is likely to be one connecting link between the two kinds of models, and it is the explanation for the fact that such a large part of scientific progress in psychiatry has had its starting point in clinical observation. It has been the insight and perception of those who could see recurring features in clinical phenomena and ignore the redundant remainder that have made the creative contribution.

Perhaps an example from a common form of affective disorder may serve to demonstrate the complementary use made of the different models in clinical practice. After investigating the patient with several anxiety symptoms, the clinician may arrive at a diagnosis of agoraphobia. In order to do this he requires a scheme of classification that derives in essentials from a medical model. And without such a scheme the many facts from different sources he assembles to complete the clinical picture, to enable him to put flesh on the skeleton, would not have come to light. The investigations reveal the panic-stricken, housebound state to have begun in the formative years, from the learning acquired and vicissitudes experienced by the individaual with a certain make-up in a special kind of familial environment. From these have sprung the traits of emotional dependence, anxiety proneness, psychosexual immaturity, the incapacity for adult tenderness and affection. And the crippling disabilities that follow the impact of stress are often the parody of traits that have been evident long before the emotional illness made its appearance.

This developmental and historical part of the formulation, which sees in emotional disorder the recrudescence of the problems first experienced in the formative years of childhood, draws upon the teachings of psychodynamics and, nowadays, also on learning theory. For the purpose of understanding and establishing effective rapport with patients, looking before and after has come to stay. But the efficacy of treatments derived from it cannot be assumed; the treatments have to be empirically tested. Notwithstanding the partially historical origins of the patient's illness, its alleviation demands treatments that have been made possible by classification and a medical model.

None of the new dimensions that have been added to psychiatry in the past fifty years would have been possible without the order introduced by classified descriptive psychiatry. Not only advances in physical treatment, but psychopharmacology and psychiatric biochemistry as well, would have failed to reach their present stage of development. The growth of psychodynamic knowledge would also have been impeded, for, although it worked in depth with individuals, it leaned upon psychiatric nosology in diagnosing melancholia, obessional illness, phobic states, and paranoid psychosis and even in adding the nosological concept of "anxiety neurosis."

For the present, unifying explanations or hypotheses that can accommodate the accounts of depression provided in psychosocial terms, as well as in the language of cerebral mechanisms, elude us. That the brain provides the substrate or final common pathway for disorders of every kind, few workers would seriously question, particularly in the light of recent advances in relation to the "reward-punishment" system (Olds and Milner 1954; Crow 1973) that enable us dimly to perceive how emotional disturbance might arise through disequilibrium or dysfunction. But this restates the problem in different terms, for the present knowledge of cerebral mechanisms provides no insight as to why some are merely unhappy and others suffer from one of the many forms of emotional disturbance. But in recent years animal models have come on the scene that may provide fruitful possibilities in investigating the association between psychodynamic, developmental, therapeutic, and possibly taxonomic aspects of affective disorder. These are discussed in the next section.

Ethological Models

In recent years certain models of human depression have been derived from ethological observations in animals. Those that have used the effects of separating infant monkeys from their mothers are of particular interest in that the patterns of behavior that follow are reminiscent of human depression. The consequences of separation of a child from its mother do not appear irrevocable, as originally supposed by Robertson and Bowlby (1952), in that the effects are markedly mitigated by the provision of a surrogate mother. But the stages in the response of the separated child are replicated by infant monkeys placed in a similar predicament. Bowlby described a stage of "protest," in which the child is restless and tearful and appears to be searching for the mother, and a stage of apathy and withdrawal, denoted as "despair," followed by "detachment," in which the mother is rejected at reunion. The first two phases are recognizable as the bereft rhesus monkeys of Hinde, Spencer-Booth, and Bruce (1966) and the pigtail monkeys of Kaufman and Rosenblum (1967), whose mothers were removed for periods of four weeks. The initial reaction of agitation with pacing, searching, head movements, restlessness, and distress calls was followed by a period in which the infant sat hunched almost rolled into a ball with its head down between its legs, unresponsive, disengaged, and almost immobile. It is noteworthy that after five or six days this "depression" entered the third phase, "recovery," in which activity and play were resumed although a month later traces of the original "grief" continued to be in evidence.

In the studies of the Harlows "protest" or "despair" predominated according to the age at which separation occurred; the former was characteristic of animals separated late, three to five years (McKinney, Suomi, and Harlow 1972; Young et al. 1973).

Seligman has recently devoted a volume to his concept of depression as a form of "learned helplessness" (1975). He found that dogs exposed to electric shocks they could neither control nor escape suffered lasting effects in their adaptive capacities. In subsequent trials they proved quite unable to terminate painful electrical stimulation by jumping a barrier to safety, a response that would have been promptly elicited from dogs not exposed to the first experiment. However, the experimental dogs, having learned that they were helpless, passively endured the painful stimulation, seemingly unable to take aversive action.

Seligman sees the loss of control over reinforcers in the environment as the central feature of clinical depression. When the indivdual becomes aware that he is powerless to influence the environment, decline in self-esteem and a state of passivity and helplessness tend to supervene. It is the loss of control that is of paramount importance; helplessness issues from the inability to manipulate environmental contingencies.

In experimental animals as in human subjects, he detects two stages in the response to danger, threat, or loss. When first exposed to such influence, an individual responds with *anxiety*. This tends to abate when the threatening factors in the environment are brought under control. However, so long as the threat continues, anxiety persists. And when threatening forces are perceived to be beyond control and action appears futile, *depression* replaces anxiety.

The author was seemingly unaware that he was paraphrasing an earlier observer. Darwin had described the relationship between anxiety and depression as follows: "After the mind suffers from a paroxysm of grief, and the cause still continues, we fall into a state of low sprits or are utterly dejected. Prolonged pain generally leads to the same state of mind. If we expect to suffer, we are anxious, if we have no hope of relief, we despair."

What forms of human affective disorder are most closely stimulated by the ethological models? If the unitary theory is adopted, they can be construed as replicating at different stages of development the whole repertoire of painful and unpleasant human emotions. However, if the affective disorders are regarded as heterogenous, they appear in a rather different light. One has to ask whether the experimental models go beyond normal responses to grief, including "frantic grief," to use a term coined by Darwin. If they are regarded as conforming closely to some pathological emotional states, which group of disorders do they resemble most closely? We find that the features of certain conditions seem to figure more prominently than those of others. No bipolar illness appears ever to have been convincingly generated, nor has cyclical mania, or cyclical depression recurring regularly long after deprivation, been described. Although suicidal behavior has been noted in animals, man is the only animal who is his own executioner. And depression and suicide exhibit a peak incidence in late life in most cultures that have been studied. McKinney's caution about characterizing the state of his deprived infant monkeys in specific clinical terms is understandable.

It is noteworthy also that in Seligman's experimental dogs anxiety was markedly prominent, and ulceration of the gastric mucosa was a common finding. The possibility arises that a variant of pathological anxiety had been replicated rather than clinical depression. Long-standing anxiety in human beings frequently progresses in phases to a state in which despondence,

Martin Roth

apathy, inactivity, and inertia are combined. Anxiety and phobic symptoms are merely dormant in such phases, for they are readily evoked by appropriate stimuli.

The main purpose of such conjectures is that they are open to refutation by observations on animals exhibiting experimental "depression." The differences in mode of response to various behavioral, pharmacological, and other physical treatments should help indicate to which affective disorders they bear the closest affinity. Such inquiries might also yield new information about the treatment of some forms of disordered affect and shed light on the biological factors governing the positive and negative correlations between the different disorders of affect represented within systems of classification.

Finally, it is inevitable that in studies devoted to classification, emphasis should have been laid on the diversity of affective disorders. But it should be noted that the picture that emerges is far removed from the traditional pigeonhole model. Such syndromes as anxiety and depression, endogenous and neurotic states, and even depression and mania are not independent of one another. They are negatively correlated and overlapping. There must, therefore, be some connecting links between many forms of disordered affect about the nature of which little is known and which have to figure on the agenda of future inquiries in psychiatry and biological science. The unity of affective illnesses in respect to certain common characters is not in conflict with the diversity that is of such crucial importance for the problems of diagnosis and classification and that has been the focus of interest in the studies to which these papers have been devoted.

Summary

1. The work of Adolf Meyer enriched the practice of psychiatry by directing attention to the multidimensional origins of mental distress and the unique nature of the problems of individual patients. But the disregard of classification by his school limited its scientific achievements. The taxonomic problems of affective disorders are in particular need of reappraisal.

2. The importance of the endogenous-neurotic issue resides in the fact that there are compelling reasons for attempting to make this distinction prior to all other diagnostic decisions. The confusion generated by the variable usage of the bipolar-unipolar concept has stemmed partly from failure to take this step.

3. A review shows the balance of evidence to favor the existence of at least two broadly distinct groups of patients with affective disorder. The "neuro-

tic" and "endogenous" affective disorders are negatively correlated rather than independent, but there is some overlap between patient groups.

4. Diagnostic difficulties arise in the minority of patients with features of both syndromes; proposals are advanced for the resolution of some of these problems in clinical practice and studies of classification.

5. Both the endogenous and the neurotic groups of disorders are heterogeneous. Studies of the classification of neurotic depressions with the aid of multivariate statistical techniques have yielded results that exhibit a considerable measure of consistency. However, the main syndromes delineated in these studies draw to some extent upon personality characteristics for which more precise criteria are needed. In the absence of such criteria a disorderly proliferation of terms has resulted in this clinical territory.

6. The neurotic group of disorders has to be differentiated into neurotic depressions and anxiety neuroses (or "anxiety depressions") on the basis of specific criteria. In the absence of this step there is evidence to suggest that populations of depressive patients in clinical and scientific practice encroach to an undefined extent upon the territory of the anxiety phobic and probably other neurotic disorders. The problems of clinical differentiation in this area have been previously discussed (Roth 1976a, b).

7. On the basis of recent observations, including the results of studies undertaken by the author and his colleagues, proposals are made for a new classification of affective disorders. This is in the form of a logical decision tree, which entails diagnostic differentiations that have to be made in succession at four hierarchical levels.

8. Certain "schizophreniform" states appear to have a kinship with affective disorder. The two main groups concerned are (a) those related by family history and long-term course to the anxiety states and (b) those with some relationship to bipolar affective disorders. They should be tentatively included in classifications of affective disorder to promote explorations of the character of the underlying relationships.

9. The models of depression required for clinical and for scientific purposes are different. The nature of the relationship between models of affective disorder conceived in terms of different dimensions is beyond the scope of present knowledge to define. Models of depression in animals studied by ethologists are more likely to be related to certain forms of affective disorder than to others. Inquiries that clarify the kinships between animal models and human illness might illuminate many issues, including those of classification.

References

Angst, J.; and Perris, C.: The nosology of endogenous depression: Comparison of the results of two studies. *Int. J. Ment. Health* 2: 145-48, 1972.

Baastrup, P. C.: Aspects of schizophrenia. W.P.A. Symposium, Yerevan, Tibisili (Soviet Union), 1973.

Bowlby, J.: Grief and mourning in infancy and early childhood. *Psychoanal. Study Child.* 15: 9-52, 1960.

Cade, J.F.J.: Lithium salts in the treatment of psychotic excitement. *Med. J. Aust.* 36: 349-53, 1949.

Carney, M.W.P.; Roth, M.; and Garside, R. F.: The diagnosis of depressive syndromes and the prediction of ECT response. *Brit. J. Psychiat.* 111: 659-74, 1965.

Cattell, R. B.: The role of factor analysis in research. *Biometrics* 21: 405-35, 1965.

Clayton, P.; Desmaris, L.; and Winokur, G.: A study of normal bereavement. *Amer. J. Psychiatry,* 125: 168-78, 1968.

Crow, T.: Catecholamine-containing neurons and electrical self-stimulation. II. A theoretical interpretation and some psychiatric implications. *Psychol. Med.* 3: 66-73, 1973.

Eighth Revision International Classification of Diseases Adapted For Use in the United States. Public Health Service Publication 1693. Washington: Government Printing Office, 1968.

Eysenck, H. J.: The classification of depressive illness. *Brit. J. Psychiat.* 117: 241-50, 1970.

Fahy, J. T.; Brandon, S.; and Garside, R. F.: Clinical syndromes in a sample of depressed patients: a general practice material. *Proc. R. Soc. Med.* 62: 331-35, 1969.

Feighner, J. P.; Robsin, E.; Guze, S. B.; Woodruff, R. A.; Winokur, G.; and Munoz, R.: Diagnostic criteria for use in Psychiatric Research. *Arch. Gen. Psychiat.* 26: 57-63, 1972.

Garside, R. F.: Depressive illness in late life (correspondence). *Brit. J. Psychiat.* 122: 118-19, 1973.

Garside, R. F.; Kay, D.W.K.; Wilson, I. C.; Deaton, I. D.; and Roth, M.: Depressive syndromes and the classification of patients. *Psy. Med.* 1: 333-38, 1971.

Gillespie, R. D.: The clinical differentiation of types of depression. *Guy's Hospital Report* 79: 306-44, 1929.

Gower, J. G.: Some distance properties of latent root and factor methods used in multivariate analysis. *Biometrika* 53: 325-38, 1966.

Gurney, C.; Roth, M.; Garside, R. F.; Kerr, T. A.; and Schapira, K.: Studies in the classification of affective disorders. II. The relationship between anxiety states and depressive illness. *Brit. J. Psychiat.* 121: 162-66, 1972.

Gurney, C.; Roth, M.; Kerr, T. A.; and Schapira, K.: The bearing of treatment on the classification of the affective disorders. *Brit. J. Psychiat.* 117: 251-55, 1970.

Hamilton, M., and White, J. M.: Clinical syndromes in depressive states. *J. Ment. Sci.* 105: 985-98, 1959.

Hill, D.: Depression: disease, reaction or posture? *Am. J. Psychiat.* 125: 445-57, 1968.

Hinde, R. A.; Spencer-Booth, Y.; and Bruce, M.: Effects of 6-day maternal deprivation on rhesus monkey infants. *Nature* 210: 1021, 1966.

Hordern, A.; Burt, C. B.; Holt, N. F.; and Cade, J.F.J. (eds.): *Depressive States: A Pharmacotherapeutic Study.* Springfield, Illinois: Thomas, 1965.

Kasinin, J.: Acute schizo-affective psychoses. *Am. J. Psychiat.* 90: 97-126, 1933.

Kaufman, I. C., and Rosenblum, L. A.: The reaction to separation in infant monkeys: analytic depression and conversation-withdrawal. *Psychosom. Med.* 29: 648-75, 1967b.

Kay, D.W.K.; Garside, R. F.; Beamish, P.; and Roy, J. R.: Endogenous and neurotic syndromes of depression: a factor analytic study of 104 cases. Clinical features. *Brit. J. Psychiat.* 115: 377-88, 1969.

Kendell, R. E.: *The Classification of Depressive Illnesses.* Maudsley Monograph No. 18. London: Oxford University Press, 1968a.

_____: The problem of classification. In *Recent Developments in Affective Disorders*, ed. A. Coppen and A. Walk. *Brit. J. Psychiatry*, Special Publ., No. A, 1968b.

Kendell, R. E.; and Post, F. Depressive illnesses in late life (correspondence). *Brit. J. Psychiatry*, 122: 615-17, 1973.

Kerr, T. A.; Roth, M.; and Schapira, K.: Prediction of outcome of anxiety states and depressive illnesses. *Brit. J. Psychiat.* 124: 125-33, 1974.

Kerr, T. A.; Roth, M; Schapira, K.; and Gurney, C.: The assessment and prediction of outcome in affective disorders. *Brit. J. Psychiat.* 121: 162-74, 1972.

Kety, S. S.; Rosenthal, D.; Wender, P. H.; and Schulsinger, F.: The types and prevalence of mental illness in the biographical and adoptive families of adopted schizophrenics. In *The Transmission of Schizophrenia*, ed. D. Rosenthal and S.S. Kety. Oxford: Pergamon, 1968.

Kiloh, L. G.; Andrews, G.; Neilson, M.; and Bianchil, G. N.: The relationship of the syndromes called endogenous and neurotic depression. *Brit. J. Psychiat.* 121: 183-96, 1972.

Kiloh, L. G.; Ball, J.R.B.; and Garside, R. F.: Prognostic factors in the treatment of depressive states with imipramine. *Brit. Med. J.* 1: 1225-27, 1962.

Kiloh, L. G., and Garside, R. F.: The independence of neurotic depression and endogenous depression. *Brit. J. Psychiat.* 109: 451-63, 1963.

Klein, D., and Daves, J.: *Diagnosis and Drug Treatment of Psychiatric Disorders*. Baltimore: Williams & Wilkins, 1969.

Klerman, G. L.; Dimascio, A.; Weissman, M.; Prusoff, B.; and Paykel, E. S.: Treatment of depression by drugs and psychotherapy. *Am. J. Psychiat.* 131: 186, 1974.

Labhardt, F.: *Die Schizophrenieähnlichen Emotionpsychosen*. Berlin: Springer, 1963.

Langfeldt, G.: The prognosis in schizophrenia. *Acta Psychiat. Scand.* 31: Suppl. 110, 1956.

Lazare, A., and Klerman, G.: Hysteria and depression: the frequency and significance of hysterical personality features in hospitalised women. *Am. J. Psychiat.* 124: 48-56, 1968.

Lazarus, A.: Learning theory and the treatment of depression. *Behav. Res. Ther.* 6: 83-89, 1968.

Leonhard, K.: *Aufteilung der Endogen Psychosen*. Berlin:1957.

Lewis, A. J.: Melancholia: A clinical survey of depressive states. *J. Ment. Sct.* 80: 277-378, 1934.

McClelland, H. S.; Roth, M.; Neubauer, H.; and Garside, R. F.: Some observations on a case-material based on patients with certain common schizophrenic symptoms. In *Proc. of the IV World Congress of Psychiatry Madrid*, ed. J. J. Lopez Ibor. Excerpta Medica Foundation, September 5-11, 1966.

McKinney, W. T.; Suomi, S. J.; and Harlow, H. F.: Repetitive peer separation of juvenile-age rhesus monkeys. *Arch. Gen. Psychiatry* 27: 200-203, 1972.

Mapother, E.: Manic-depressive psychosis. *Brit. Med. J.* 2: 872-76, 1926.

Maxwell, A. E.: Multivariate statistical method and classification problem. *Brit. J. Psychiat.* 119: 121-22, 1971.

Mendels, J., and Cochrane, C.: The nosology of depression: the endogenous-reactive concept. *Am. J. Psychiat.* 124: 1-11, 1968.

————: Depressive factors and response to electroconvulsive therapy (to be published).

Montaigne, M. de: *Essais*. Edited and annotated by A. Thibaudet (Bibliotheque de la Pieiade). Paris: Gallimard, 1950.

Moran, P.A.P.: The establishment of a psychiatric syndrome. *Brit. J. Psychiat.* 112: 1165-71, 1966.

Olds, J., and Milner, P.: Positive reinforcements produced by electrical stimulation of septal area and other regions of rat brain. *J. Comp. Physiol. Psychol.* 47: 419-27, 1954.

Paykel, E. S.: Classification of depressed patients: a cluster analysis derived grouping. *Brit. J. Psychiat.* 118: 275-88, 1971.

Paykel, E. S.; Dimascio, A.; Haskell, D. et al.: Effects of maintenance amitriptyline psychotherapy on symptoms of depression. *Psychol. Med.* 5: 67-77, 1975.

Perris, C.: A study of bipolar (manic depressive) and unipolar recurrent depressive psychoses. *Acta Psychiat. Scand.* 42: Suppl. 194, 1966.

_____: The heuristic value of a distinction between bipolar and unipolar affective disorders. In *Classification and Prediction of Outcome of Depression.* (Symp. Scho. Reinhartshausen/Rhein, Sept. 1973), 1974a.

_____: A study of cycloid psychoses. *Acta Psychiat. Scand.,* Suppl. 253, Munksgward, Copenhagen, 1974b.

Post, F.: The management and nature of depressive illness in late life: a follow-through study. *Brit. J. Psychiat.* 121: 393-404, 1972.

Robertson, J., and Bowlby, J.: Responses of young children to separation from their mothers. *Courrier Centre Inter. Enfance.* 2: 131-42, 1952.

Rosenthal, S. H.: Neurotic and endogenous depression: a skeptical view. *Brit. J. Psychiat.* 113: 1154-55, 1967.

Rosenthal, S. H.; and Gudeman, J. E.: The endogenous depressive pattern: an empirical investigation. *Arch. Gen. Psychiat.* 16: 241-49, 1967a.

_____: The self-pitying constellation in depression. *Brit. J. Psychiat.* 113: 485-98, 1967b.

Rosenthal, S. H.; and Klerman, G. L.: Content and consistency in the endogenous depressive pattern. *Brit. J. Psychiat.* 112: 471-84, 1966.

Roth, M.: The borderlands of anxiety and depressive states and their bearing on new and old models for the classification of depression. Paper presented at a symposium on neurotransmission and disturbed behaviour, organized by the Interdisciplinary Society of Biological Psychiatry, Amsterdam, May 20-22, 1976. For inclusion in a volume to be published by Dr. Evven F. Bohn, B. V. Haarlem, Netherlands, 1976a.

_____: The association of affective disorders and psychosomatic disease and its bearing on certain problems of psychosomatic medicine. Paper presented at the 3rd Congress of the International College of Psychosomatic Medicine, Rome, September 1975, 1976b.

Roth, M.; Gurney, C.; Garside, R. F.; and Kerr, T. A.: Studies in classification of affective disorders. I. The relationship between anxiety states and depressive illness. *Brit. J. Psychiat.* 121: 147-61, 1972.

Roth, M.; Gurney, C.; Mountjoy, C. Q.; Kerr, T. A.; and Schapira, K.: The relationship between classification and response to drugs in affective disorders: problems posed by drug response in affective disorders. In *Ciba Found. Symp. 39.* New York: Elsevier, 1976.

Rummel, R. J.: *Applied Factor Analysis.* Evanston: Northwestern University Press, 1970.

Sandifer, M. G.; Wilson, I. C.; and Green, L.: The two-type thesis of depressive disorders. *Am. J. Psychiat.* 123: 93-97, 1966.

Schapira, K.; Roth, M.; Kerr, T.; and Gurney, C.: The prognosis of affective disorders: the differentiation of anxiety states from depressive illness. *Brit. J. Psychiat.* 121: 175-81, 1972.

Seligman, M.E.P.: *Helplessness.* San Francisco: W. H. Freeman & Co., 1975.

Slater, E.; and Slater, P.: A heuristic theory of neurosis. *J. Neurol. Psychiat.* 7: 49-58, 1944.

Strömgren, E.: Reactive psychoses. *Acta Jutlandica* 40: 4, 1968.

van Praag, H. M.: Biological psychiatry in perspective: the dangers of sectarianism in psychiatry. V. Some inferred trends. *Comprehensive Psychiatry* 13: no. 5, 1972.

Welner, J.; and Strömgren, E.: Clinical and genetic studies of benign schizophreniform psychoses based on a follow-up. *Acta Psychiat. Neurol. Scand.* 33: 377-99, 1958.

Wolpe, J.: Neurotic depression: experimental analog, clinical syndromes and treatment. *Amer. J. Psychother.* 25: 362-68, 1971.

Young, L. D.; Suomi, S. J.; Harlow, H. F.; and McKinney, W. T.: Early stress and later response to separation. *Am. J. Psychiat.* 130: 400-405, 1973.

VII

THE PSYCHOBIOLOGY
OF AFFECTIVE STATES:
THE LEGACY OF ADOLF MEYER

Gerald L. Klerman *

Introduction

Following the revelations of the Flexner Report, Johns Hopkins University committed itself to creating the first modern American medical school. In this monumental work, Osler, Halsted, and the other greats of the Hopkins faculty were joined by Adolf Meyer, who set about to create the first university teaching center in psychiatry in North America.

In Meyer's achievement there were two paradoxes. The first paradox was that the new Hopkins medical faculty brought to American medicine the clinical and research approaches of the European medical schools, particularly those based upon the German tradition of experimental biology. Meyer evolved a uniquely American approach to psychiatry based on the American philosophic school of pragmatism and a dynamic psychology rooted in life experience and social context rather than laboratory experimentation. The second paradox in this achievement was that Meyer was not a native American, having been born in Switzerland in 1866 and emigrating to the United States at the age of 26.

In this interpretation I follow Lidz, who states,

*Administrator/Alcohol, Drug Abuse, and Mental Health Administration/Department of Health, Education and Welfare/and Professor of Psychiatry/Psychiatry Service/Harvard Medical School/Boston, Massachusetts

115

> According to Zilboorg and Henry, Meyer introduced the best tradition of European psychiatry into the American scene. This is a gross misapprehension . . . he created an uniquely American orientation into psychiatry.

Originally trained in neurology and neuropathology, Meyer gradually came to regard these fields as less and less relevant to psychiatry. In the image of Darwin and Huxley, he evolved his own approach, which he called *psychobiology*, in which biology is conceived of not as laboratory experimentation, but as the study of living persons adapting to their environment and ecological biology.

Lidz, Henderson, Muncie, and Lief emphasize the extent to which Meyer, though trained in European medicine, was profoundly influenced by the emerging pragmatic school of philosophy. Soon after coming to the United States, Meyer was in touch with John Dewey, Charles Pierce, Paul Caras, and William James, whose writings and teachings were to transform American higher education via their ideas of pragmatism in the first American school of philosophy. At the same time Meyer was active with the early Chicago social psychologists, George Herbert Mead and Charles Cooley and with the Boston group of psychologists, William James, Morton Prince, Hugo Munsterberg, and Boris Sidis. This infusion of new psychological and philosophical ideas contributed to Meyer's own psychobiological approach to the understanding of man in relation to this environment. To quote Wendell S. Muncie, Adolf Meyer's view of psychobiology was based on the principle that

> "the living man can only be studied as a whole person in action."

This view of psychobiology is probably not the connotation of psychobiology as laboratory research, nor is it the current usage of psychobiology in psychology as research on brain mechanism in perception, cognition, sexuality, learning, or other aspects of psychological development and behavioral functioning.

The special meaning Meyer gave to psychobiology to other common and technical words represents one of the serious obstacles that contemporary psychiatrists have with Adolf Meyer writings.

Meyer is seldom read and even less frequently understood. The great impact of Meyer was not through his writings on any specific theory or even a comprehensive system but rather through his general approach and through the pervasive influence that his students had on medical education, on residency training, and on psychiatry's clinical and therapeutic approaches to patients.

As I shall explicate later, Meyer emphasized the role of experience, in its broadest sense, as contributing to the adaptation of the person to his environment. He viewed biology in its broadest Darwinian evolutionary sense as ecology, but he did not specify the particular aspects of experiences relevant to mental illness or its treatment. He proposed a general approach. His students identified specific areas for research and therapeutic practice. Lemkau, Pasamanick, Rennie, and Leighton researched social epidemiology. Campbell, Muncie, Frank, and other clinicians contributed to the humanization of American psychiatry to encompass concern with family life, child development, schools, juvenile delinquency, psychosomatic medicines, public health, and the first efforts at preventive psychiatry and mental hygiene.

Valuable as these efforts have been in broadening and humanizing psychiatry in America, their scientific impact has been disappointing. Research efforts to demonstrate the importance of the social and familial environment in the etiology and epidemiology of mental illness have yet to produce compelling evidence. Efforts to demonstrate the efficacy of dynamic psychotherapy in children, adolescents, and adults have been few in number and until very recently unimpressive as to magnitude of therapeutic outcome (Frank et al. 1965).

I come to this conclusion with personal disappointment; I regard the hypotheses generated by Meyer and his students as intellectually stimulating and socially innovative. Nevertheless, hypothesis generating without hypothesis testing leaves unfulfilled the scientific promise of any field, especially psychiatry. The Meyerian approach, although it has had many important humanistic gains, has recently reached a considerable scientific impasse. The advent of the new psychopharmacologic approaches has strengthened the neurobiological approach to psychiatry. In contrast, research to establish environmental and family hypotheses about schizophrenia, depression, and neuroses has faltered. The use of standardized interview schedules, rating scales, and statistical techniques for diagnosis and classification have revived previously discarded approaches to psychopathology. These and other developments have placed the Meyerian approach on the intellectual defensive.

In view of these new forces I propose the time is appropriate for a reassessment of Meyer's psychobiology. In the light of recent scientific history it is desirable that there be a modification of Meyer's original psychobiological concepts and a revision of the directions that some of Meyer's students gave to his teachings.

In the body of this paper I will clarify my understanding of the Meyerian approach in psychiatry and where it has yet to achieve its scientific promise. I will use the area of research on the affective disorders, depression and mania, as a specific illustration of these dilemmas and conclude with my own reappraisal of Meyer's psychobiology.

The Meyerian Approach to Psychiatry

As Theodore Lidz, in his 1966 Adolf Meyer Lecture to the American Psychiatric Association on the occasion of the centennial of the birth of Adolf Meyer, stated,

> For most psychiatrists, Adolf Meyer has become little more than a name; an honored and even revered name—although they may be uncertain why. Of course he is the founder of psychobiology, but what does this term that is defined so variously mean?

Meyer is not read much these days. When I was preparing this paper and started to reconstruct Meyer's intellectual development, I went to the Harvard medical library and had an experience similar to that described by Lidz.

> When I borrowed the volumes of his collected papers from the Yale and Stanford libraries, the binding still crackled when opened and the pages were still crisp and virginal, unblemished by pencil.

Athough Meyer is remembered only vaguely by contemporary American psychiatrists, his influence, though unacknowledged except in the vaguest form, is still discernible albeit indirect.

Meyer was unqualifiedly the preeminent American psychiatrist between the two world wars. William Allanson White in 1933 said,

> Dr Meyer has been the outstanding influence in the development of psychiatry in this country. For about 40 years, practically no major enterprise has been projected in the field of psychiatry which he has not influenced in some way.

Meyer's influence was exerted mainly through his role as Phipps Professor at the Johns Hopkins Medical School. He created the first enduring American academic department of psychiatry, and the Phipps Clinic remained the center of academic psychiatry in the United States until World War II. His students became the leading professors of psychiatry and the writers of the most influential textbooks in America and in Great Britain.

Most important, his approach to psychiatry permeates all of American psychiatric teaching and practice and much but not all of its research.

The Meyerian Approach. What was the Meyerian approach? I have identified a number of basic principles.

1. The psychiatric patient was looked upon as a unique person. Again to quote Lidz,

> I believe that his influence remained very much alive not only in his students but in virtually all of American psychiatrists. It enters into the way we talk to our patients and conceptualize their problems and how we think about personality development and the nature of psychiatric disorders; and indeed and why we are interested in the person and his life experience rather than so many of our continental colleagues primarily in a disease process.

2. The importance of life experience was emphasized. As Henderson said,

> It was not one factor which Meyer considered important but all factors, sexual, social, and environmental which must always be considered in relation to the life of the individual. Meyer was concerned with the total personality in his environmental setting. It was this comprehensive viewpoint that constituted so great a departure from the formal descriptive methods which had preceded it.

3. There was a tendency to depreciate heredity and genetics.

> He was always most strongly drawn to considerations of habit formation, training and education than he was to the hereditary-genetic aspect. The hereditary factor was almost too negative an approach for him.

4. Descriptive symptomatology and diagnoses were downgraded. Again quoting Henderson.

> He [Meyer] wanted something more lasting than the rigid symptomological nosology of the Kraepelian school. Mere delineation of symptoms did not expose the facts in relation to the life situation which Meyer regarded as essential.

These four principles form the core of the Meyerian approach: humanistic, individualistic, ecological, and comprehensive, it represents an approach born of neurology and pathology but transformed into psychology and clinical therapeutics.

It has been stated that Meyer's

> strong interests in anatomy and pathology of the human brain was to have an abiding influence on his ultimate commitment to clinical psychiatry.

The content of these statements is true but does not capture the essence of Meyer's career direction. Meyer was born near Zurich, Switzerland, in September, 1866, and received his medical training at the University of Zurich. Shortly after graduating from medical school, he spent time in Scotland, where he became acquainted with the views of British empiricism. He came to the United States at the age of 26 and gained further training in neurology and neuropathology. He worked as a pathologist, first at a state hospital in Kankakee, Illinois, then at Worcester State Hospital in Massachusetts, and then in New York at the New York State Psychiatric Institute.

Between his arrival in the United States at the age of 26 in 1892 and his assumption of the Henry Phipps Clinic leadership in 1913, a time span of less than twenty years, Meyer rapidly rose to a position of major leadership within American psychiatry. These were the decades in which he moved out of the pathology laboratory and into clinical psychiatry. He became knowledgeable with the leaders of emerging American pragmatic philosophy, the social psychology of Cooley and Mead, and the new psychotherapy of Morton Prince and William James at Harvard. This was the period when he wrote his comprehensive and scholarly critiques of Kraepelin's concept of dementia praecox, and he strove to formulate a dynamic psychology independent of but sympathetic to the rapidly expanding and powerful impact of Sigmund Freud, Carl Jung, and the other psychoanalysts.

The impact of Meyer's ideas was not fully felt until after World War II, when his students became the leading teachers and academics as chairmen of departments of psychiatry and textbook writers.

Meyer gave only the broadest outline of the important role of experience for the development and treatment of mental illness. His students carried his ideas forward into various areas—

1. The child guidance movement of 1920 bore his influence. With the creation of these clinics there was the hope and the promise that early intervention would correct neurotic habits and prevent the later emergence of schizophrenia, delinquency, and other serious adult disorders.

2. His philosophic commitment to breaking down the dualism of mind and body contributed to the early development of psychosomatic medicine, particularly through Stanley Cobb at Massachusetts General Hospital and Eugene Meyer, who developed the liaison service at Hopkins.

3. His work on dynamic psychotherpay with Morton Prince later bore fruit in the pioneering studies of psychotherapy by Jerome Frank.

4. Although he was cautious about psychoanalysis, his approach actually stimulated the growth of the neo-Freudian modifications of classic psycho-

analysis. Writing in the *American Handbook of Psychiatry* of the various schools of psychoanalysis, Mora said,

> Rado, Horney, Sullivan, and Fromm typify the original American contribution to the psychoanalytic movement although all of them, with the exception of Sullivan, were European-born. Their work has taken place almost exclusively in this country, and they have almost all been influenced by the Swiss born Adolf Meyer, founder of the school of psychobiology, which had considerable impact on American psychiatry probably because of its optimistic view of human nature in contrast to Freud's pessimism. . . . Large numbers of pupils eventually acquired leading academic positions in this country as well as abroad. Aside from its eclectic orientation and broad acceptance, psychobiology is generally considered to have facilitated the introduction of the psychoanalytic movement in this country.

5. The Baltimore-Washington area became the center for new social psychiatric ideas. In the period before and during World War II Hopkins and the Washington-Baltimore area were the loci of great intellectual ferment with the infusion of insights from anthropology, sociology, and the other social sciences into psychiatry and psychology. These ideas became crystallized in Sullivan's interpersonal theory of psychiatry.

6. Sullivan and Fromm-Reichman and their associates at the Chestnut Lodge and Sheppard and Enoch Pratt hospitals initiated a psychotherapeutic approach to schizophrenia.

7. Among the most lasting contributions of Meyer will be the vision of a social epidemiology of mental illness. Lemkau, Pasamanick, Rennie, Leighton, and others amplified Meyer's general approach to identify social factors that generate mental illness and mental retardation in specific communities. Starting from the surveys in the eastern health district in Baltimore through the Midtown-Manhattan project in New York and the Nova Scotia studies, new hypotheses of social epidemiology were generated. The momentous Midtown-Manhattan project attempted to assess the impact of urban life inhabitants. Leighton, one of the first behavioral scientists, first studied the impact of concentration camp experience on the Japanese internees in California and then—in a brilliant series of world-wide projects—studied the Yoruka in Nigeria, the Eskimos in northern Canada, and the Navaho in the southwest United States and, in his classical study, assessed the impact of socioeconomic change on the social structure and organization of an otherwise stable community in Sterling County, Nova Scotia.

8. In public health Meyer's influence was equally powerful, but here, too, it stands in danger of being forgotten. In 1913 he proposed the blueprint for

a mental hygiene clinic for the area near the hospital, and this succinct plan captures the essence of today's community mental health center program.

> I consider it of the greatest importance that the clinic make itself responsible for the mental health of a fairly well circumscribed unit of population, so as to make possible studies of the social situation and of the dynamic factors which lead to the occurrence of mental derangements which must be attacked for purposes of prevention.

Taken together, these areas constitute an impressive legacy. The efforts of Meyer's students in these areas transformed American psychiatry and ultimately psychiatry throughout the world. Psychiatry teaching and scholarship were broadened by additions from philosophy, social science, and epidemiology. Clinical practice became humanized and more socially responsive and more oriented toward public health.

But what of research and theory? These are the long-term investments for any professions. How have mental health research and psychiatric investigations prospered in the legacy of Adolf Meyer?

The Disappointing State of Some Current Psychiatric Research. In reviewing the psychiatric research in the past twenty years that has been developed in the areas listed, I conclude on a disappointing note. The hypotheses have been imaginative, even brilliant, but their testing has not been conclusive. We are no closer to conclusive evidence that family experience is relevant for the etiology for schizophrenia than when Lidz and Fleck first proposed this hypothesis. A role for social stress in the epidemiology of mental illness remains an imaginative hypothesis, but the data of the Midtown-Manhattan and Nova Scotia studies did not provide risk factors or even rates of incidence and prevalence of specific disorders, such as schizophrenia, depression, mental retardation, or anxiety states. Early intervention in childhood, through the child guidance movement, has not proved to be efficacious in the prevention of adult psychoses or juvenile delinquency. Psychotherapy of schizophrenia and manic-depressive illness offers little promise of being demonstrated as effective or efficient.

Although the hypotheses generated have been imaginative and creative and the efforts initiated to test their validity have been provacative, the research too often does not meet the current criteria of adequate controls, independent observations, and use of advanced statistical measures. The reasons for this disappointing state are only in part methodological. I believe the main reason is a conceptual one: a failure to specify the nature of the dependent variables, the clinical psychopathology. If we regard current psychiatric research as a grand experiment, Meyer and his students enlarged the scope of the independent variables relevant to psychiatry. Our predecessors in the nineteenth century had demonstrated that infection, trauma, intoxicating drugs, the endocrines, and genetics were relevant independent variables. Meyer proposed that experience, social stress, family dynamics, and early childhood experience were potentailly equally important; but setting up research to demonstrate that these factors are independent variables requires attention to the dependent variable—psychopathology—and this variable has not been given sufficient detail and appropriate attention.

In their zeal to bring a humanistic concern to the needs of individual patients, Adolf Meyer's students came close to throwing the medical model out of psychiatry and perhaps even moving psychiatry out of medicine into social work. So fearful were some psychiatrists of the adverse consequences of diagnostic labeling that they denied the validity of illness groups as scientific constructs and the utility of differential diagnosis as an essential clinical skill to be learned by psychiatric residents and medical students.

The principle that each patient was a unique person was pitted against the scientific necessity of placing patients into groups, categories, and classes on the basis of specific attributes. Carried to its logical extreme, this antidiagnostic view has been crystallized in sociology as "labeling theory" by such writers as Scheff and Rosenhan; and within psychiatry there have emerged the "antipsychiatrists," particularly Szasz and Laing.

It may be unfair to place on the legacy of Adolf Meyer or his students the sins of the labelers and the antipsychiatrists. However, as I trace the intellectual history of modern psychiatry, I am impressed by the impact and consequences of Meyer's influential critique of Kraepelin's "Dementia Praecox" (*ARNMD*, 1910) and Sir Aubrey Lewis's parallel critique of the classification of depression in his influential papers on melancholia (*Journal of Mental Science*, 1933). These papers and the textbooks that incorporated their views argued against the concepts of disease and classification. They proposed the uniqueness of the individual patient and the need to search for a multitude of diagnostic factors in order to understand each case. They blurred the distinction between the abnormal and the normal.

These were commendable humanistic influences. They counteracted the cold, indifferent, and remote stance of a generation of narrowly somatic alienists of the late nineteenth century. From the research point of view, however, they have proved to be inhibitors of progress; a medical specialty built upon the uniquesness of each individual case cannot generalize or communicate. Each time we make decisions as to which kind of patient will do well in what kind of psychotherapy or drug, we are placing patients in some kind of group.

The Meyerian approach tended to unify all mental illness and to group patients together. Much of mental health epidemiology in the postwar period tended to use general disability scales or symptom checklists and thereby to discuss a mental illness as a single entity. While the rest of medicine was specifying discrete disorders by defining homogeneous clinical groups validated against biological correlates, mental illnesses were grouped together into a single whole, and attempts at defining subgroups or redefining psychopathologic criteria were disparaged (Menninger, *The Vital Balance*, 1953).

The scientific promise of the Meyerian approach will not be fulfilled and social factors and personal experience established as relevant independent variables until the dependent variables—the clinical disorders—are specified with greater precision. New research on psychopathology has reestablished the validity of the medical model in psychiatry. If there is to be a new Meyerian approach to psychiatry, it must unite the relevance of social factors as the independent variables with the new precision of psychopathology as the dependent variables.

Let me illustrate my conclusions by attention to certain aspects of the psychobiology of depression and the affective states.

The Meyerian Approach to Depression and the Affective States

In 1970 at the Annual Meeting of the American Psychopathologic Association, of which Adolf Meyer was one of the founding members, at a meeting devoted to disorders of mood, I stated that "therapy and research have progressed but ideas and theories about depression have lagged. Many terms and concepts remained rooted in experiences derived from the era prior to World War II." This is particularly evident in discussions of clinical characterization of depression. In reviewing the state of research on depression, I have found it useful to place current difficulties into historical perspective. The term *depression* evolved its current meaning in this century and in large part because of Adolf Meyer's desire to replace the previously popular term *melancholia*. Meyer was concerned that the term *melancholia* was applied narrowly to patients who were severely psychotic and also that it implied a theory of etiology dating back to the ancient Greek notions of humors and temperaments. The early formulations of Freud in *Mourning and Melancholia* (1917) and those of Kraepelin in *Manic Depressive Insanity* (translated into English in 1921) were derived from their observations of patients who were both depressed and psychotic. Their concern was with the differentiation of normal states from psychotic ones.

One of Kraepelin's major achievements had been the separation of manic-depressive insanity from dementia praecox. The majority of patients whom he studied were both psychotic and institutionalized; and for the psychiatrist of that era the main clinical problem was to distinguish the psychotic from the nonpsychotic, the institutionalized from the noninstitutionalized.

Over the succeeding decades psychiatry rapidly expanded its boundaries beyond the mental hospital, and Adolf Meyer played a vital role in fostering what he called "extramural psychiatry." World War I hastened the attention given by the public and by government to mental illness, and Meyer was active along with Clifford Beers and Thomas Salmon in the formation of the National Committee for Mental Hygiene, the forerunner of the National Association for Mental Health. Increasing attention became focused on the many nonpsychotic affective conditions seen in the private consultation offices, the newly developed outpatient clinics, and the new public health facilities. Among the clinical disorders seen with increasing frequency were the various depressions, and considerable clinical debate was precipitated over the best descriptions and groupings for the many patients being seen who were increasingly young, less severely ill, and neurotic—that is, nonpsychotic. Only a small minority met the classic criteria of manic-depressive insanity with loss of reality testing as manifested by delusions, hallucination, and other impairments of perception, cognition, memory, or orientation. Yet the existing concepts, both descriptive and psychodynamic, had been developed mainly from institutional settings. As a partial attempt to resolve this issue, Gillespie (1929) proposed a distinction between the endogenous, or autonomous, forms of depression and the reactive, or neurotic, disorders; this separation gained wide prominence, particularly in Great Britain.

In this confused situation, Aubrey Lewis published a series of three papers between 1933 and 1935. Lewis had recently returned to Britain from a period in the United States, where he had spent time first at the Phipps Clinic in Baltimore and then at the Boston Psychopathic Hospital where C. McPhee Campbell, previously at Hopkins, was the superintendent and also professor of psychiatry at Harvard Medical School.

In this set of papers, which derive from Lewis's M.D. thesis, he is explicit about his adoption of the psychobiological approach and his rejection of existing nosological efforts, including those of Kraepelin, Gillespie, and others. Lewis' papers on depression represent the application of the Meyerian principles to the affective disorders in a manner almost directly parallel to Meyer's earlier critique (1908) of the dementia praecox concept.

My review of the history of theory and research in depression leads me to conclude that Lewis' position became dominant in practice, teaching, and research. Until the late 1950s the Meyerian view of depression guided thinking and investigation.

This Meyerian approach to depression, as epitomized by Lewis's writings, emphasized both underlying unity and diversity among patients with various depressions. Depression was seen as within the range of human experience, the psychobiological reaction of the person to life's vicissitudes. Classifications and subdivisions were rejected, particularly those that emphasized genetic or other biological factors. Meyer, Lewis, and their colleagues did acknowledge gradations from major to minor disturbances and from acute to chronic, but such groupings as manic-depressive psychosis or the endogenous-reactive typology were criticized as unsubstantiated scientifically and ethically dangerous.

These criticisms had both scientific and moral aspects. From the scientific aspect, Meyer, Lewis, and their students questioned the adequacy of the data for group separation. They regarded the existence of cases with mixed features as sufficient to invalidate hypotheses as to subgroups. In essence, this critique is a statistical one, but only recently have advanced multivariate statistical techniques and computer technology been brought to bear on the problem by such investigators as Roth, Kendell, Hamilton, and Kiloh in England and Grinker, Overall, and Klerman in the United States.

The Meyerian critique of classification is also a moral critique, essentially that of the consequences of labeling. Students of Meyer have been concerned with the adverse psychological, social, and ethical consequences of labeling people as psychiatrically ill. They argue that such diagnoses as "psychotic" or "manic depressive" initiate an adverse series of events for the patient, who becomes stigmatized, depersonalized, and regarded as untreatable or incurable and therefore worthy only of institutionalization or shock treatment.

These views were dominant teachings in American psychiatry in the era after World War II, and I suspect they are views held by the majority of clinicians and practitioners. The emphasis was on the uniqueness of the individual and the multiplicity of factors of personal experience, family background, and psychodynamics involved in any depressed patient's illness. If many factors were involved, they were all potentially of equal weight, but in practice and theory only lip service was given to biological considerations. The end result was highly individualized diagnostic and treatment practices and almost a moratorium on clinical research in depression. This discouraging situation reversed itself dramatically in the late 1950s and early 1960s following a series of developments that changed the theoretical approach and clinical practice in depression. There were five developments—

1. the advent of new psychotherapeutic drugs, particularly the tricyclics, the MAO inhibitors, and lithium;
2. rapid advances in neurochemistry, neuropharmacology, and neuroendocrinology;
3. new evidence for genetic transmission of selected affective disorders;
4. the application of quantitative methods to descriptive psychopathology, diagnosis, and nosology;
5. research on loss in the early childhood experience of future depressives and as a precipitating event for the acute episode.

Let me briefly discuss each of these developments.

As regards the advent of the new psychotropic drugs relatively little need be said, since this development is now well known. The significance of these developments is not only their dramatic impact on therapeutic practice but also the significant improvement they stimulated in the quality of clinical psychiatric investigations. The double-blind, placebo-controlled, randomized, clinical trial has now become established as the standard design for studies of the efficacy of new drugs. The power of this research design increasingly has become incorporated in evaluations of treatments other than drugs, including individual psychotherapy, group teachings, behavior therapy, and even community mental health practice.

The advent of clinical psychopharmacology represents a dramatic and illustrious chapter in the recent history of psychiatric research and therapeutic practice, but in celebrating its impact we should not forget that there was a marked resistance in the profession to the introduction of these drugs. As Swazey and others have documented, in the 1950s the ideological position of the profession was antibiological, and the use of these new drugs was the subject of controversy for almost a decade. Even today there are large numbers of psychiatrists who tell their patients, "I don't believe in drugs" and who resist learning about their modes of action and therapeutic usefulness.

Parallel with the therapeutic research on these new drugs were rapid advances in neurochemistry, neuropharmacology, and neuroendocrinology. The outstanding quality of these investigations provides a valuable bridge between clinical efficacy studies of drugs and basic laboratory advances in the neurosciences.

Since the late 1960s there has been a renaissance of psychiatric genetics. After a period of inactivity around World War II genetic studies of the affective disorders have gained new momentum, particularly following the independent documentation by three research groups of probably genetic modes of transmission in manic-depressive patients. Simultaneously in the late 1960s Winokur and associates in St. Louis, Perris and associates in Sweden, and Angst in Switzerland undertook family studies of manic-depressive patients. They divided their clinical groups into unipolar and bipolar types of recurrent affective disorders following Leonhard's amendment of Kraepelin's concept of manic-depressive illness.

This was an impressive convergence of the finding of these three research groups, especially since they made use of the same nosological principle. The importance of these genetic-familial investigations was heightened by clinical trials, which demonstrated that the unipolar-biopolar distinction was a powerful predictor of response to medication, particularly lithium for manic and bipolar depressed patients and lithium and tricyclics for recurrent unipolar patients. This convergence of genetic and therapeutic findings utilizing the unipolar-biopolar diagnosis has convinced most skeptics of the importance of a diagnostic approach that recognizes the heterogeneity of the affective disorders, rather than the unitary approach that had dominated clinical practice and research for so many decades.

The hypothesis of heterogeneity within the affective disorders was further supported by quantitative studies of symptom assessment using rating scales. Data derived from rating scales have been subjected to advanced statistical analysis, particularly such techniques as factor analysis and clustering techniques. We are on the verge of new standards for diagnostic practice. Psychiatric diagnosis has been criticized as unreliable and invalid. Recent studies—especially the NIMH-CIB Collaborative Study of Depression in St. Louis, Iowa, New Haven, and Boston—demonstrate that when standard interview techniques, such as those developed by Spitzer and Endicott, are combined with systematic training of observers and a determination to give due value to symptomatology and phenomenology, high rates of reliability in diagnosis and concurrence among observers emerge.

Building upon Meyer's general interest in the role of experience, clinicians developed a number of hypotheses as to the importance of loss and separation during early childhood as a predisposing factor and as an immediate precipitating event for the acute depression. Only recently have adequately designed studies using control groups and quantitative techniques been applied to testing these hypotheses. The preliminary results indicate that although such events do occur with greater frequency among depressives than in the general population, they do not occur universally. Only about 15 to 20 percent of adult depressives had experienced manifest loss or separation in childhood, and among adult depressives, loss or separation as a precipitating event occurred in only about 25 percent of patients in the six months prior to the onset of the clinical state. There is good but not compelling evidence that these experiential factors are important contributors to the pathogenesis of the depressed state, but they are not necessary factors or universal causes. One cannot support an exclusively environmentalistic or experiential theory of depression, at least not on the basis of the available evidence. Given these limitations, many theorists and investigators, particularly those with strong biological orientations, have been tempted to discard the hypotheses related to loss, early experience, personality, or family dynamics. While the research in this areas has been slow to develop adequate standards and the findings to date are far from compelling, the disappointments thus far do not preclude further investigations in this area. What is important is that we acknowledge the weakness of the evidence for these hypotheses compared to the growing strength of the evidence in pharmacology, genetics, and psychopathology.

Taken together, these lines of investigation indicate the value of a pluralistic approach to the affective disorders. The concept that the affective disorders form a single continuum cannot be accepted with as much consensus as was the case a decade ago. Of all the investigators who have used advanced statistical techniques, only Kendell interprets the evidence as supporting the continuum concept. All other investigators have concluded that the depressions likely represent a heterogenous group of syndromes and that they probably are of multiple etiologies.

The most useful conceptual model is the classic model that evolved in the eighteenth and nineteenth centuries. In this model the affective disorders are like the other grand syndromes in medicine—anemia, congestive heart failure, or jaundice. They are a final common pathway of altered pathophysiology that manifest themselves with common clinical features in symptomatology and behavior. Moreover, they are likely to involve multiple etiologies. In the case of depression, we know that some states are due to such drugs as reserpine, aldomet, or corticosteroids. The bipolar manic-depressive illnesses are probably due predominantly to genetic factors, but even here heterogeneity seems to be indicated, according to Winokur's data. Perhaps other forms of depression are due to the consequences of early experience, maladaptive personality features, and social stress; but these hypotheses remain unverified.

My assessment of the state of research on depression is, I believe, consistent with Meyer's early concepts of psychobiology and his generally skeptical view toward the dogma.

While I have concluded that the current state of research attempting to verify Meyerian approaches has failed to fulfill its promise, I have not concluded that the approach is basically in error. Where the disappointment comes is not with the nature of the hypotheses generated or with Meyer's conception of the biological adaptation of a man in relationship to his environment, but rather with the failure of investigators in the Meyerian tradition to employ the principles of experimental controls and quantitative assessments and to incorporate the principles of psychopathology and advances of statistics. In fact, it is my conviction and expectation that, when these studies utilizing these techniques are brought to bear upon the hypotheses generated from Meyer's concept of experience, new theoretical integrations will emerge.

References

Angst, J.: Etiological and nosological considerations in endogenous depressive psychosis. In *Monographien aus dem Gesamtgebiet der Neurologie und Psychiatrie*. Berlin: Springer, 112, 1966.

Frank, J. P.; Stone, A. R.; Hoehn-Saric, R.; Ember, S.; and Nash, E. Some situational factors associated with responses to psychotherapy. *Amer. J. Orthopsychiat.* 35: 682-87, 1965.

Gillespie, R. D.: The clinical differentiation of types of depression. *Guy's Hospital Report* 79: 306-44, 1929.

Hale, N. G., Jr.: *Freud and the Americans*. New York: Oxford University Press, 1971.

Hall, J. K.: *One Hundred Years of American Psychiatry*. New York: Columbia University Press, 1944.

Hamilton, M.: A rating scale for depression. *J. Neurol. Neurosurg. Psychiat.* 23: 56-62, 1960.

Hamilton, M., and White, J.M.: Clinical syndromes in depressive states. *J. Ment. Sci.* 105: 985-98, 1959.

Henderson, D. K.: Introduction to *Collected Papers of Adolf Meyer. II. Psychiatry*, ed. E. E. Winters. Baltimore: Johns Hopkins Press, 1951.

Kendell, R. E.: *The Classification of Depressive Illnesses*. Maudsley Monograph No. 18. London: Oxford University Press, 1968.

Klerman, G. L.: Clinical research in depression. In *Disorders of Mood*, ed. J. Zubin and F. D. Freyhan. Baltimore: Johns Hopkins Press, 1972.

Klerman, G. L., and E. S. Paykel: Depressive pattern, social background and hospitalization. *J. Nerv. Ment. Dis.* 150: 466-78, 1970.

Lewis, A.: Melancholia: a historical review. *J. Ment. Sci.* 80: 1-42, 1934a.

————: Melancholia: a clinical survey of depressive states. *J. Ment. Sci.* 80: 277-378, 1934b.

————: States of depression: their clinical and aetiological differentiation. *Brit. Med. J.* 2: 875-78, 1938.

Lidz, T.: Adolf Meyer and the development of American psychiatry. *Am. J. Psychiat.* 123: 320-32, 1966.

Lief, A.: *The Commonsense Psychiatry of Adolf Meyer.* New York: McGraw-Hill, 1948.

Menninger, K.: *The Vital Balance.* New York: Viking Press, 1953.

Meyer, A.; Jelliffe, S. E.; and Hoch, A.: *Dementia Praecox.* Boston: Richard G. Badger, 1911.

Mora, G.: Recent psychiatric developments since 1939. In *American Handbook of Psychiatry*, 2nd edition, ed. S. Arieti. New York: Basic Books, 1974.

Muncie, W.: *Psychobiology and Psychiatry.* St. Louis: C. V. Mosby, 1948.

_____ : The psychobiological approach. In *American Handbook of Psychiatry*, 2nd edition, ed. S. Arieti. New York: Basic Books, 1974.

Perris, C.: A study of bipolar (manic-depressive) and unipolar recurrent depressive psychoses. *Acta Psychiat. Scand.*, Suppl. 194: 1-189, 1966.

Robins, E.; Munoz, R. A.; Martin, S.; and Gentry, K. A.: Primary and secondary affective disorders. In *Disorders of Mood*, ed. J. Zubin and F. A. Freyhan. Baltimore: Johns Hopkins Press, 1972.

Roth, M.; Gurney, C.; Garside, R. F.; and Kerr, T. A.: Studies in the classification of affective disorders I. The relationship between anxiety states and depressive illnesses. *Brit. J. Psychiat.* 121: 147-61, 1972.

Winokur, G.; Clayton, P.; and Reich, T.: *Manic Depressive Illness.* St. Louis: C. V. Mosby, 1969.

Wittenborn, J. R.: Reliability, validity, and objectivity of symptom-rating scales. *J. Nerv. Ment. Dis.* 154: 79, 1972.

Zung, W.W.K.: A self-rating depression scale. *Arch. Gen. Psychiat.* 12: 63-70, 1965.

SELECTED BIBLIOGRAPHY
PERTAINING TO ADOLF MEYER

Adolf Meyer Memorial. *Bulletin of the Johns Hopkins Hospital* Suppl. 1: 89, 53-80, 1951.

Blass, E. M. (ed.): *The Psychobiology of Curt Richter*. Baltimore: York Press, 1976.

Lief, A.: *The Commonsense Psychiatry of Dr. Adolf Meyer*. New York: McGraw-Hill, 1948.

Muncie, W. (ed.): *Psychobiology and Psychiatry: A Textbook of Normal and and Abnormal Human Behavior*. Foreword by A. Meyer. St. Louis: C. V. Mosby, 1939.

Winters, E. E. (ed.): *The Collected Papers of Adolf Meyer*. Vol. 1. Neurology. Vol. 2. Psychiatry. Vol. 3. Medical Teaching. Vol. 4. Mental Hygiene. With a complete bibliography of works by Adolf Meyer. Baltimore: Johns Hopkins Press, 1950-52.

Winters, E. E., and A. M. Bowers (eds.): *Psychobiology: A Science of Man*. Springfield, Ill.: C. C. Thomas, 1957.

NOTES ON CONTRIBUTORS

FLOYD E. BLOOM is Director of the Arthur V. Davis Center for Behavioral Neurobiology at the Salk Institute in La Jolla, California. He was trained in medicine at Washington University, did postdoctoral work in pharmacology, psychiatry, and anatomy at Yale, and was Chief of the Laboratory of Neuropharmacology at the National Institute of Mental Health before assuming his present position in 1975.

JOSEPH V. BRADY is Professor of Behavioral Biology at The Johns Hopkins University School of Medicine and Director of the Division of Behaviroal Biology in the Department of Psychiatry and Behavioral Sciences. He lectures on the experimental analysis of behavior to medical and premedical students at Johns Hopkins and actively conducts research in behavioral pharmacology and behavioral physiology.

SEMOUR S. KETY is presently Professor of Psychiatry at the Harvard Medical School and Director of the Mailman Psychiatric Research Center at McLean Hospital in Belmont, Massachusetts. He holds the M.D. and Sc.D. degrees from the University of Pennsylvania and served as Scientific Director of the National Institutes of Mental Health and Neurological Diseases and Blindness before becoming Henry Phipps Professor and Director of the Department of Psychiatry at The Johns Hopkins University School of Medicine in 1961.

GERALD L. KLERMAN is Professor of Psychiatry at the Harvard Medical School and Administrator of the Alcohol, Drug Abuse, and Mental Health Administration of the Department of Health, Education, and Welfare. He has been Director of the Connecticut Mental Health Center at Yale and the Erich Lindemann Mental Health Center at Harvard and has served as Deputy Chief of the Psychiatry Service at Massachusetts General Hospital.

BEATRICE C. AND JOHN I. LACEY are both Fels Professors of Psychiatry in the School of Medicine at Wright State University. Their productive research collaboaration at the Fels Research Institute of Antioch College goes back well over a quarter century, and their contributions in the area of experimental psychophysiology have been widely acclaimed in both academic and professional circles.

EUGENE MEYER, III is Professor of Psychiatry and Professor of Medicine at The Johns Hopkins University School of Medicine. He received his medical training at Johns Hopkins and was among the last of the students to whom Adolf Meyer lectured at the Henry Phipps Psychiatric Clinic. He has published extensively on the training and research opportunities presented by psychiatric consultation on medical and surgical wards.

NEAL E. MILLER has been Professor at Rockefeller University in New York City since 1966, following a distinguished period of tenure at Yale as James Rowland Angell Professor of Psychology. His widely published research in the areas of experimental and physiological psychology has importantly influenced the development of laboratory and clinical applications involving biofeedback.

MARTIN ROTH is Professor and Chairman of the Department of Psychiatry, New Addenbrooke's Hospital, University of Cambridge, Cambridge, England. He was the First President of the Royal College of Psychiatrists and has co-authored a world famous text on clinical psychiatry. Before accepting his present post, Dr. Roth was Professor of Psychological Medicine, University of Newcastle-upon-Tyne, for over twenty years.

EDWARD J. SACHAR is Professor and Chairman of the Department of Psychiatry at Columbia University College of Physicians and Surgeons and Director of the New York State Psychiatric Institute. He received the M.D. degree from the University of Pennsylvania in 1956, received postdoctoral training at the Harvard Medical School, and served as Chairman of the Department of Psychiatry at Albert Einstein College of Medicine before assuming his present position in 1976.

INDEX

137

The Johns Hopkins University Press

This book was composed in IBM Press Roman text and Compugraphic English Times display type by Culpeper Publishers. It was printed and bound by Thomson-Shore, Inc.

Library of Congress Cataloging in Publication Data

Main entry under title:
Research in the psychobiology of human behavior.

Based on papers presented as a part of the Adolf Meyer Symposium on Psychobiology, Johns Hopkins University, 1976.
Bibliography: p. 133
Includes index.
1. Psychobiology–Congresses, 2. Human behavior–Congresses. I. Meyer, Eugene,
1915-   II. Brady, Joseph V. [DNLM: 1. Psychophysiologic disorders.
2. Mental disorders. WM100.3 R432]

QP360.R45   616.8'5   78-24710
ISBN 0-8018-2238-6

Date Due